Date Due

o 38-297

The International
Bond Market
in the 1960's

PRAEGER SPECIAL STUDIES IN
INTERNATIONAL ECONOMICS AND DEVELOPMENT

The International Bond Market in the 1960's

ITS DEVELOPMENT AND OPERATION

John F. Chown
Robert Valentine

FREDERICK A. PRAEGER, Publishers
New York · Washington · London

The purpose of the Praeger Special Studies is to make specialized research monographs in U.S. and international economics and politics available to the academic, business, and government communities. For further information, write to the Special Projects Division, Frederick A. Praeger, Publishers, 111 Fourth Avenue, New York, N.Y. 10003.

FREDERICK A. PRAEGER, PUBLISHERS
111 Fourth Avenue, New York, N.Y. 10003, U.S.A.
5, Cromwell Place, London S.W. 7, England

Published in the United States of America in 1968
by Frederick A. Praeger, Inc., Publishers

Library of Congress Catalog Card Number: 68-28471

Printed in the United States of America

ACKNOWLEDGMENT

The authors have benefited from the help and advice of many individuals and institutions, both for providing statistics and for making helpful suggestions as the book progressed. In particular, we should like to thank the following for their invaluable aid: W. J. Hopper of S. G. Warburg & Company Limited; Julius Strauss of Strauss, Turnbull & Company; S. M. Yassukovitch of White Weld & Company; Walter Damm of the E.E.C. Banking Federation; and Hans and Ulrich Bär of Julius Bär & Company, Zurich. Last, but not least, we are indebted to our indefatigable secretary, Miss Pamela Mesnard, for typing the manuscript.

CONTENTS

Page

ACKNOWLEDGMENTS v

LIST OF TABLES xi

Chapter

1 THE RISE OF THE INTERNATIONAL BOND MARKET 1

Early History and Definitions 1
    Euro-bonds and Euro-dollars 4
The Role of the United States 8
The United Kingdom as an Entrepôt
    Market 10
Other European Markets and Holding-
    Company Centers 14
Concluding Remarks 17
Notes to Chapter 1 19

2 TYPES OF BOND ISSUES AND USUAL FEATURES 21

Location of the Subsidiary 21
Currency of the Issue 24
    Single-Currency Loans 24
    Optional-Currency Loans 28
    Parallel Loans 29
    Unit-of-Account Loans 30
Convertible Loans 34
Warrant Issues 36
Time-Guaranteed Notes 38
Usual Features and Guarantees 40
    Sinking Funds 42
    Optional Redemption 44
    Tax Provisions 45
    Currency Devaluation 48
Explanatory Tabular Information 49
Notes to Chapter 2 55

3   RAISING FINANCE ON THE INTERNATIONAL
    BOND MARKET   57

    The Pure Holding Company   58
    The Debt-to-Equity Ratio   59
    Tax Considerations in Luxembourg   61
    The Offering Prospectus   64
    Stock-Exchange Listings   66
    Underwriting   68
    The Importance of After-Markets   76
    Notes to Chapter 3   77

4   RESTRICTIONS ON THE MOVEMENT OF
    INTERNATIONAL CAPITAL AND EFFECTS
    ON THE MARKET   79

    Background Information   79
    The Interest-Equalization Tax   81
    The Voluntary Guidelines Program   83
    Exchange Control Acts in the
        United Kingdom   86
    The Remainder of the Sterling Area   95
    The European Economic Community   97
        Belgium and Luxembourg   100
        France   100
        Germany   101
        Italy   103
        The Netherlands   103
    The European Free Trade Association   104
        Sweden   104
        Switzerland   104
    Notes to Chapter 4   106

5   THE TAX TREATMENT OF INTEREST AND
    THE ROLE OF THE HOLDING COMPANY   108

    Background Information   108
    The Role of the Subsidiary   110
    Double-Tax Agreements   113
    An Examination of Various National
        Practices   115
        Switzerland   115
        The Netherlands   117

        Luxembourg   119
        The United States   120
        Special Problems of a United
          Kingdom Parent   120
        Special Problems of Issuers in
          Other Countries   122
    A Summary of National Laws   123
        The United States   123
        The United Kingdom   124
        France   126
        Austria   127
        Belgium   127
        Denmark   127
        Finland   128
        Germany   128
        Greece   128
        Ireland   129
        Italy   129
        Luxembourg   129
        The Netherlands   130
        Norway   130
        Portugal   130
        Spain   130
        Sweden   130
        Switzerland   131
    Withholding Taxes on International
      Dividends   131
    Notes to Chapter 5   136

6   THE ECONOMIC IMPACT OF THE MARKET   137

    Introduction   137
    The Euro-Dollar Market   138
        Definition of the Euro-Dollar   139
        Examples of the Euro-Dollar Market   140
    The Euro-Bond Market   143
    The U.S. Balance of Payments   144
    The U.K. Balance of Payments   147
    Effect on Exchange Rates   148
    Effect on Interest Rates   149
    The General Effect on Capital Markets   156
    Notes to Chapter 6   158

Chapter   Page

7   RECENT DEVELOPMENTS AND THE FUTURE OF
    THE MARKET   159

    Introduction   159
    The New U.S. Regulations   160
    The Market Itself   163
    The Euro-World   166
    The International Company   168
    Notes to Chapter 7   173

STATISTICAL APPENDIX   177

ABOUT THE AUTHORS   189

LIST OF TABLES

Table		Page
1	Publicly Floated International Bonds	5
2	Examples of International Offerings, 1966	6
3	All Forms of International Issues, 1962-66	7
4	Public International Bond Issues, 1962-66	25
5	Unit-of-Account Issues, 1961-66	32
6	Classification by Types of Issue, 1962-66	51
7	Classification by Nationality of Issuer, 1962-66	52
8	Withholding-Tax Rates on Portfolio Dividends	132
9	Withholding-Tax Rates on Dividends Paid to Stockholders with Substantial Participation	134
10	Long-Term European Government-Bond Yields, 1965-66	153
11	Foreign-Bond Resume	177
12	All International Bonds Issued, 1965-66	180

The International
Bond Market
in the 1960's

CHAPTER **1** THE RISE OF THE
INTERNATIONAL
BOND MARKET

EARLY HISTORY AND DEFINITIONS

The 1960's have been a decade of fast and furi-
ous development in international financial markets.
A whole new terminology has arisen, exemplified by
such phrases as "Euro-bonds," "Euro-dollars," and
"Euro-sterling"; and the emphasis of finance has
shifted from the national to the international
scene (despite misguided efforts by several governments to stimulate the contrary flow). In such an
environment, many of the changes have inevitably
been far-reaching, and both the theorist and the ad-
ministrator have found it exceedingly difficult to
keep up-to-date. Universities in general have
lagged behind in education, mainly because the new
techniques have thus far remained the preserve of
dedicated professionals. In any case, the liaison
between theory and practice in international finance
has never been good.[1]

The purpose of this book is to fill one such
gap between theory and practice. Inevitably, the
major emphasis will be on the latter field, not
only because facts are incontrovertible but also
because it is in this area that education is most
required. We shall not really be concerned with
the theoretical details, because the arguments on
this score, where not self-evident, are controversial. However, we shall attempt to point out broad
general conclusions, particularly in Chapter 6,
which discusses the wider economic implications of
the new markets.

That considerable education is required is indicated by this quotation from a talk by Frank Manheim of Lehman Brothers:

> the American borrower is uncomfortable
> insofar as the European bond market
> baffles him. The distribution of debt
> securities in the U.S., their after-
> market, their trading volume etc. are
> all so understandable and visible so
> to speak, in the large and highly or-
> ganised, as well as regulated American
> markets, that the American issuer feels
> lost when he tries to comprehend what
> to him is incomprehensible. He gives
> up trying, after hearing endless refer-
> ences to "Kuwait money," the "Swiss
> Accounts," etc. Nevertheless he must
> have the money, so he plunges ahead
> with a pitiful demonstration of trust
> and faith in his investment banker.
> He becomes inured to . . . the com-
> plexity and frustrating mystery of
> European financing.[2]

In general, this book will attempt to unravel
the complexity and ease the frustration of international financing. In particular, its topic is
the international bond market.

Broadly, an international bond is defined as a
loan issued in a country (or countries) where the
borrower is not resident. The borrower can be a
government, a government-guaranteed enterprise, an
international organization (such as the World Bank),
or a company. The currency of the loan will not
necessarily be that of the borrower's or lender's
country of origin but will be dictated by various
considerations. In fact, the loan can be issued
simultaneously in several currencies, or with the
option of subscribing in several currencies, or
indeed, in units of account that are a sort of
supranational foreign exchange. (See Chapter 2.)

Table 12 (Statistical Appendix) provides a comprehensive list of all public international bond issues during 1965 and 1966. The principal source of this data was the Banking Commission of the European Economic Community, who defines international bonds as follows:

Issues of public companies, when the actual issue is effected:

1. In the market of a country other than that of the borrower and in a currency other than that of the borrower

2. In both the market and currency of the borrower where, due to particular circumstances, the shares cannot be sold there (for example, issues by United States companies via United States subsidiaries)

3. In both the market and the currency of the issuer, where part or all of the issue is placed abroad by an international syndicate

4. In units of account, or carrying a currency option

Issues made by international organizations, even if these organizations are considered as domestic by the authorities of the country in which they are resident and even if the issue is made on the domestic market, excluding the following:

1. In the case of parallel issues, the tranche issued on the domestic market of the borrower (in domestic currency)

2. The issues on the domestic stock exchange of the subsidiary of a foreign company when the issue is denominated in domestic currency and the following conditions apply, that the shares can be sold on the domestic stock exchange, and that an important element of the issue is guaranteed by the parent company

At this stage, many of the above terms may not be comprehensible to the reader, but the full definition has been supplied for completeness, and it is hoped that the terms will become clear as the reader progresses. It will also become apparent that much confusion reigns over the precise definition of an international bond, and we have supplied the broadest definition.

For example, a Canadian Government issue made available in Canada (in Canadian dollars) is clearly not an international bond, although of course, a certain number of subscriptions come from abroad. On the other hand, some recent Australian Government issues in United States dollars qualify, as do many issues by foreign subsidiaries of such U.S. companies as International Harvester, Pepsi-Cola, and Honeywell.

In general, an international issue is characterized by three factors. First, the issue will be made in countries other than the resident country of the principal borrower. Second, the currency of the loan will be related to international rather than domestic financial considerations. And third, the loan will be specially designed to appeal to the largest class of international investors from the tax point of view; for example, there will be no withholding tax on interest payments.

Such bonds are often called "Euro-bonds" or international bonds, and we propose to employ either nomenclature. Strictly, the phrase "Euro-bonds" refers to the large volume of U.S. dollar issues made in Europe and excludes some types of international issue, but common usage has inaccurately extended to all forms of international issue. The term "Euro-dollar" has suffered the same fate with the result that much needless confusion has arisen.

Euro-bonds and Euro-dollars

At this stage, it is well to dispose of one further source of confusion, that between Euro-bonds and Euro-dollars. A Euro-bond, as explained

above, is a certain type of international loan,
while Euro-dollars constitute interest-bearing deposits in U.S. dollars at banks outside the United
States. Euro-bonds usually have a term of five to
twenty years for maturity; Euro-dollars are often
purely call-money, and in any case rarely extend
beyond two years. In other words, a Euro-bond is a
long-term funded instrument, while a Euro-dollar is
a short-term deposit. It is true that Euro-dollars
are often used for short-term financing and underwriting of Euro-bond issues; the implications of
this are examined in Chapter 6. In a sense, they
constitute the shorter end of an integrated international money market. But they were in existence
long before Euro-bonds, and the distinction must be
clearly kept in mind.

We intend, therefore, to devote our attention
to the international bond market, where the growth
in activity over the past few years has been phe-
nomenal. Table 1 gives an indication of this growth;
Table 2 shows the spread of issues, with ten examples of international offerings in 1966; Table 3
includes all forms of international issues for the
years 1962-66.

TABLE 1

Publicly Floated International Bonds*

Year	Amount (in millions of U.S. dollars)
1960	230
1961	520
1962	650
1963	580
1964	990
1965	1,180
1966	1,500**

*Excludes private placings, as well as Israeli,
United Kingdom Commonwealth, Canadian, and World
Bank issues.

**Estimated.

Source: "Report on Western Europe," New York:
The Chase Manhattan Bank, No. 40 (March-April, 1966).

TABLE 2

Examples of International Offerings, 1966

Month of Issue	Country	Issue	Currency
February	Italy	SGI International Holdings, S.A.	U.S. Dollars
February	Norway	Redernes Skibskreditforening	Units of Account
March	Germany	Thyssen Investment, S.A.	German DM
March	Ireland	Ireland (7%, 1976-81)	Sterling German DM
March	New Zealand	Government of New Zealand (6-1/2%, 1976-86)	U.S. Dollars
March	South Africa	Highveld Steel & Vanadium Corporation	German DM
April	Mexico	Comission Federal de Electricidad	Units of Account
July	Europe	Transalpine Finance Holdings, S.A.	U.S. Dollars
July	United Kingdom	Beecham International Holdings, S.A.	U.S. Dollars
July	United States	General Electric Overseas Capital Corporation	German DM

TABLE 3

All Forms of International Issues, 1962-66
(in millions of U.S. dollars)

Year	Public	Private	Total
1962	766.3	249.3	1,015.6
1963	796.6	369.4	1,166.0
1964	1,327.8	193.7	1,521.5
1965	1,682.8	269.5	1,952.3
1966	1,968.8	120.0	2,088.8

Source: Banking Commission of the European Economic Community, June, 1966, and March, 1967.

Apart from the countries mentioned in Table 2, international bonds have also been issued on behalf of Australian, Austrian, Belgian, Danish, Finnish, French, Icelandic, Israeli, Jamaican, Japanese, Dutch, Philippine, Portuguese, Swedish, and Venezuelan concerns, and the currencies employed have ranged from those in Table 2 to Swiss francs, French francs, Belgian francs, Italian lire, and Dutch florins.

Of course, international bond issues are not new. In fact they have been in existence since the early nineteenth century. Paul Einzig says:

> There was in each of the principal lending centres and also in small countries such as Holland, Switzerland, Belgium and Sweden, an investing public accustomed to subscribe to foreign bond issues, and it was encouraged to do so by the stable monetary conditions prevailing between the battle of Waterloo and the first battle of the Marne.[3]

In those days, in fact, expertise was by no means
lacking, and governments were not so concerned with
imposing restrictions upon international business.
Exchange control was virtually unknown, and taxes
on transfers, issues, and coupons were low.   In
addition, as Einzig points out, the major lending
countries had favorable balance-of-payments posi-
tions, a condition that by no means applies today.

THE ROLE OF THE UNITED STATES

After World War I, foreign issue business continued, with an inevitable gravitation toward Wall
Street.   But the Wall Street crisis had a severe de-
terrent effect, and the continuing depression in
the 1930's, together with newly awakened fears about
currency stability and the promises of governments,
reduced new foreign issue business to a trickle.
This state of affairs more or less continued until
recent years owing to the hangover from World War II
and the tightening of exchange control and other
fiscal restrictions (to say nothing of taxation).
Indeed, many governments including the United Kingdom were actively opposed to such issues at the
time.[4]

The United States remained the major country
for the issue of such international issues as ex-
isted, principally due to the relatively low level
of U.S. interest rates and the affluence of investors.   This is not to say, of course, that the principal buyers of these issues were all U.S., but the
U.S. provided a convenient underwriting, primary,
and secondary market.

At this stage, before turning to recent developments, it is well to dispose of several fallacies
concerning the international bond market and to
outline the broad principles of its operation.
Such a bond usually runs from fifteen to twenty
years, is usually issued around par at an interest
rate dictated by international considerations, and
carries various guarantees as to principal, interest, future tax, and future exchange control by the

parent company or government. As mentioned earlier, the currency of the issue may be a single currency, several currencies, or units of account, provided that such currency is mutually acceptable to the borrower and the lender. Various safeguards against the devaluation of the reference currency are available, the most obvious being the unit-of-account bond. This will be explained in detail in Chapter 2, but in general the unit of account, defined in terms of seventeen reference currencies, minimizes the risks to both borrower and lender that arise in a normal currency loan if the exchange rate of the designated currency is revalued or devalued.

It is important to realize that the currency of the loan may not necessarily bear any relation to the creditor country, the borrowing country, or the country of issue. Originally, the currency was related to the country in which the loan was issued, but this distinction no longer applies. Indeed, most modern international bonds are issued in several countries simultaneously and bought by investors of many countries; and the borrowing entity may not be unique (for example, Transalpine Finance). So the loans are truly multicurrency and international, being managed by a world-wide syndicate of underwriters, and the market of issue may be purely an entrepôt market, that is, one which lends to foreign borrowers capital owned by nonresident investors.[5]

The above distinction between international issues and national, foreign issues is most important and is often ignored by statistics. While, as mentioned previously, foreign bond issues are not new, the idea of international syndication is a recent major development. Robert Genillard of White Weld and Company, a leading authority on international bond issues, stated: "Most statistics on international bond flotations . . . lump together foreign issues floated internally without a conscious effort to distribute them world-wide, with those which are internationally syndicated and sold simultaneously in many countries," and he defined

the true international bond market as one "in which
investors deal in bonds which represent for most of
them foreign assets and where the final primary
claim on the borrower is almost always to be made
outside the legal jurisdiction of the holder of the
bonds."[6]

Consequently, it does not really matter where
the loan was officially issued, nor does the fact
that it is listed on one particular stock exchange
imply that many investors of that country are bondholders. Claudio Segré, a leading European expert
on international bonds, noted:

> For example, the London quotation has
> almost a symbolic character in view of
> the high cost of operations on that
> market; the subscription for and de-
> livery of the securities takes place
> in Luxembourg, for tax reasons among
> other things; the financial service
> is effected in the principal European
> centres as well as, frequently, in
> New York. The laws that govern rela-
> tions between the issue, the consortium
> and the bondholders are those of the
> issuer's country or those of Luxem-
> bourg; last, but not least, the securi-
> ties are always placed with residents
> of countries other than Great Britain
> where the premium that has to be paid
> to obtain investment dollars makes the
> purchase of such securities of little
> interest.[7]

THE UNITED KINGDOM AS AN ENTREPÔT MARKET

Returning to historical trends, it has been
noted above that for many of the postwar years the
United States was the principal issuing and entrepôt
market. But this state of affairs began to change
in the late 1950's when some issuing syndicates were
organized in Europe, and this process gathered steam
in the early 1960's.

In 1963, the first U.S. dollar bond issued outside the U.S. for a non-U.S. borrower was underwritten by a Belgian-managed syndicate. At the same
time two other major factors promoting this form of
business arose. First, in mid-1963, the U.S. announced their notorious interest-equalization tax,
which totally eliminated the favorable costs of
U.S. based borrowing. Broadly this tax imposed a
15 per cent charge (later increased) on any U.S. investor purchasing a non-U.S. loan or investment;
thus, the interest rate that had to be offered to
tempt U.S. investors into international bonds had
to rise appropriately, and the interest rates ruling
in major European centers became more attractive.

Second, the major London merchant banks, beginning to realize the potential of London as an
entrepôt market, especially when the interest-
equalization tax (IET) was announced, began to take
an active interest in these issues. European groups
of underwriters were formed, and the issues were
placed easily in such countries as Switzerland without any aid from the U.S. underwriters (or investors)
whatsoever. The existence of Luxembourg as a holding company center (to be discussed later) aided
this process.

The market continued to grow in the period
from 1963 to 1965 (Table 1) with European underwriters and issues taking an increasingly active
part. In the first quarter of 1963, foreign securities issues in European markets approximated $93
million; in the last quarter they were $234 million. [8]
The system received a further jolt in mid-1965 when
U.S. corporations descended en masse on European
markets to raise capital, having been asked to limit
their capital exports out of the U.S. in order to
aid the ailing U.S. balance of payments.

These companies formed overseas subsidiaries
(usually in Luxembourg) to raise money, and the
issue was accomplished in Europe by an international
syndicate of underwriters. From virtually zero in
1963, such issues leapt to astronomical heights in

1966. The Chase Manhattan Bank acidly commented in April, 1966: "Within the last nine months, some 30 American corporations have raised a total $639 million by floating international bonds, not in New York, but in supposedly capital-starved Europe."[9]

More recently, U.S. borrowers have discovered that they can avoid interest-equalization tax (as well as withholding tax and the voluntary guidelines) equally effectively if they make their issues via a U.S. subsidiary that derives 80 per cent or more of its income from non-U.S. sources. Such subsidiaries are usually incorporated in Delaware, but the bonds are still retailed by an international syndicate. Another recent development has been the issue of short-term guaranteed notes running for a period of approximately five years. In September, 1966, Goodyear International Finance (a subsidiary of Goodyear Tire-Rubber Company) issued $20 million of such notes. The issuing syndicate included Dillon, Read and Company and the Deutsche Bank, and quotations of the notes were in Frankfurt and Luxembourg. More recently, Honeywell International Finance also made a note issue ($15 million, guaranteed notes 1969-71, unconditionally guaranteed by Honeywell Incorporated). The breadth of the distribution is evidenced by the fact that the paying agents are located in New York, London, Brussels, Paris, Frankfurt, Amsterdam, Milan, and Luxembourg.

Thus, it is clear that international-bond activity has fairly blossomed over the past few years. And the benefits to the borrowers in this market have been obvious. Furthermore, the expansion of international financing has widened the base of investor thinking, tapped new sources of cash, created a wealth of financial expertise (particularly in Europe), and brought money to many concerns with a minimum of trouble. Indeed, the financing of issues such as Transalpine Finance, involving many oil companies and the construction of a vital pipeline over the Alps, would have been virtually impossible without the efficient machinery of this market.

In addition, international-bond operations
have been beneficial to world economies in many
other ways. First, the impact on the U.S. economy
has been undeniably good, because such bonds have
contributed to a reduction in the long-term capital
outflows that have been the bane of the U.S. balance
of payments in recent years; and this still holds
true despite the recent gaps that have developed
and the switching from American shares into international bond issues. Second, the decentralization
of raising capital from New York to Europe is un-
doubtedly a good move, for obvious reasons. Finance
thereby becomes more international, resources are
more evenly allocated, and most important of all,
the U.S. is left in peace to formulate her own
monetary policies.

To borrowing countries and corporations the
advantages are also obvious. Foreign-exchange holdings are replenished, and capital is diverted to
where it is needed most. Of course, in some cases,
capital will go to the wrong places, and some countries will use such moneys to postpone the solution
of internal economic ills. Nevertheless, on balance, the flow of capital is more beneficial now
than it was when the U.S. had a deficit on external
account and lent money while Germany did not know
what to do with its surplus. The advantages to investors of this market are principally these of
portfolio diversification, devaluation hedging, and
maximum net yield.

On the debit side, there have been many complaints that the market is being slowly strangled
by U.S. subsidiary financing. (In Chapter 6, we
argue that this is unfair, particularly if it is
suggested that such operations were wholly responsible for the upward trend in European interest rates
that was evident in 1965-66.) Clearly, the market
has been congested from time to time, but such congestion brings its own solution. A pause in operation was evident in mid-1966. In addition, the
mechanism for the utilization of European liquid
funds, having been set in motion, will gather speed

as time progresses. Strauss, Turnbull, leading
London brokers on the international bond market,
have estimated that interest payments on the loans
outstanding as of March, 1966, will total $175 mil-
lion per annum, while sinking-fund repayments will
grow to the same figure in 1970, and to over $200
million in 1975. This factor alone could provide
new financing of some $350 million per annum in a
very short period of time.

Certainly operations appear to have picked up
after the mid-1966 pause. Total 1966 issues finally reached around $1.5 million excluding certain
issues (see Table 2), a 25 per cent increase in
1965, while a fair estimate of 1967 issues is about
$1.7 million. The upward trend in international
financing appears to have re-established itself.

At this stage, it is sufficient to emphasize
that the international bond market is likely to be
a permanent and useful adjunct to the financial
scene, and industrialists should make it their business to exploit this market to the fullest extent
possible. It is not necessarily true that international bonds, having been born of such restrictions as the interest-equalization tax, will vanish
as soon as fiscal restrictions vanish. Finance of
necessity must become more international, and national boundaries must become less important. If a
U.S. industrialist wishes to expand in Europe, he
should logically tap the more than adequate capital
available in Europe. In order to do this, he must
know much more than he does at present about the
conditions he is likely to encounter there. With
this in mind, we will survey the current state of
European capital markets, and in particular, the
entrepôt market that has grown up in London.

OTHER EUROPEAN MARKETS AND
HOLDING-COMPANY CENTERS

Apart from London, which will be discussed
later, the major European markets constitute Belgium, Germany, and the Netherlands. Luxembourg and

Switzerland are to some extent special cases, and
the former is discussed in Chapter 3; the Swiss
markets tend to be virtually closed to foreigners,
owing to exchange control restrictions, although
some progress toward more liberalization was made
recently.[10]

To international and particularly U.S. eyes,
European capital markets have many faults: Share
markets are narrow, expenses of financing are heavy,
and companies, investors, and institutions at times
seem totally to ignore market developments. Institutions in particular are often prohibited from buying reasonable quantities of securities owing to
national legislation, and investors prefer to leave
their money on deposit rather than buy shares. The
one outstanding feature of U.S. markets that is not
mirrored in Europe is the wide degree of share ownership; and the one major fault of European capital
markets is the lack of institutional support.
Apart from the United Kingdom, most companies prefer to obtain funds from institutions rather than
the market, just because the institutions do not
support the market.

Another major problem is the differing tax and
company law structure in each country. At present,
in fact, there is no such thing as a European capital market, owing mainly to the distortions created
by the above factors. Such tax differences as the
fact that Luxembourg levies no withholding tax
while Belgium levies 18.2 per cent affect capital
flows and more harmony is required in this respect.
The advent of the European Economic Community
should, of course, help matters, but much remains
to be done.

In a massive report, the European Economic Community published the following summary:

> Less progress has been made with the
> development of a European capital
> market than with the other elements
> of the economic union being established

in the Community. Today, the reforms
already under consideration to improve
the functioning of the capital markets
in certain member countries offer a
chance of laying the foundations of a
wider market; the focussing of effort
on this wider market seems indeed to be
a condition for the success of these
reforms, as the present shortcomings of
the capital markets are due not so much
to insufficient savings as to the impos-
sibility of adjusting correctly supply
and demand on markets that are too
narrow.[11]

As soon as European governments become more international in their outlook, the basis for an efficient capital market will be laid. After all, savings are more than adequate, this being evidenced
by the fact that the rate of increase in savings
over the past few years in European Economic Community (EEC) countries has been greater than the rate
of increase in their average gross national products.
But what is happening is that these savings are going to institutions (not to the capital market) and
are in turn being used for long-term lending to corporations (not in equities). In the period 1960-65,
net new equity issues in EEC countries increased by
an average of 6.3 per cent per annum, but net debt
increased by 21 per cent per annum in the same
period.

However, the outlook is slowly moving from the
national to the international scene. The rules governing equity investments by institutions are gradually easing, tax policies are becoming more harmoni-
ous, and the stimulus of new horizons introduced,
inter alia, by the techniques of international-bond
financing are all contributing to a more efficient
and international outlook. At the same time, the
increased capital needs of European countries are
making market reforms increasingly necessary, and
in the economic field, it is to be hoped that the
soaring interest rates and generally gloomy

industrial conditions that characterized the 1960's are gradually ending.

Certainly the impact of the international bond market has and will contribute considerably to the greater efficiency of European capital markets. The international links established by financial institutions and the new techniques this market has introduced have been wholly beneficial. Perhaps from time to time the activities of U.S. subsidiaries have been too intense, but they cannot be wholly blamed for the rising trend in European interest rates over the past few years (see Chapter 6).

CONCLUDING REMARKS

In the late 1950's, the chances of a major U.S. company raising long-term finance in Europe were slim; now, however, via the international bond market and the increased sophistication it brings in its train, the prospects are much better. Paradoxically, they are also better for European companies. The U.S. company will almost certainly come to Luxembourg (discussed in detail in Chapter 3), but it could raise finance by this method in any other country. The problems of European capital markets indicate that unless a company uses the familiar Luxembourg route, it will face many problems. Even if it does use the Luxembourg route, the fact that the bonds will be issued throughout Europe and the world by an international group of underwriters makes it imperative that the peculiarities of European capital markets be understood. Of course, international bonds markets have their own peculiarities.

The London market is a law unto itself, and the United Kingdom's entrepôt system must be studied closely. Clearly the United Kingdom is not a capital market in the international sense. The flow of domestic savings is not sufficiently adequate, sterling as a currency is somewhat under a cloud, and the balance-of-payments situation does

not exactly inspire confidence. In addition, exchange control regulations are strict, and residents who wish to buy foreign issues are subject
to severe penalties. What they must do is purchase
investment or "premium" dollars in order to pay for
these securities. This currency arises solely from
the sale of such securities by United Kingdom residents, and consequently a special market exists in
investment dollars, the "pool" being limited. In
addition, the premium is often substantial, rising
to 30 per cent or more above the strict sterling to
dollar exchange rate, owing to the relative popularity of hard currency securities and the technical
reason that, on sale, 25 per cent of investment
dollars received must be surrendered at the official rate.

Thus, United Kingdom residents not only have
to pay about 20 per cent over the odds; they also
lose about 5 per cent as a sales tax. It inevitably follows that investor interest in foreign issues
is slim. Consequently, this factor, combined with
the disadvantages mentioned above, means that despite its long and honored financial history, London cannot rank as a full-scale capital market.

However, London has many of the advantages of
a capital market. It has an efficient network of
financial institutions, well-versed in international affairs; it has a first-class stock exchange
and an excellent foreign-exchange market; as a
Euro-dollar center it possesses first-class credit
facilities. So it is natural that London should
assume an entrepôt role, that is, a role in which
the whole amount of capital lent by the United
Kingdom is contributed by nonresidents, and any
minor part acquired by residents does not affect
the balance of payments (via the premium dollar
market). In other words, London acts as a most
efficient intermediary between the borrower and the
lender.

As mentioned before, the problem of the country of issue is not vitally important, except in

the sense that the local techniques and expenses
must be known, to the U.S. or foreign borrower. In
these days of international syndication, the ultimate provider of funds, even in a true capital market, can be far-distant from the place of issue.
Sources of finance are discussed in greater detail
in Chapter 3, where considerable emphasis is placed
upon the role of Swiss and Middle East money; but,
as far as technicalities are concerned, the borrower
does not really care who the ultimate lenders are.
He must, however, ensure that an efficient dealing
market is established in one (or more) centers, and
stock-exchange listings are desirable.

As far as underwriting is concerned, the borrower need have no fears. In the international
bond market, the term "underwriting" is usually
used in the strict sense, that is, the underwriters
actually purchase the bonds at an agreed discount,
and it is up to them to find a home for the issue.
As soon as the underwriting syndicate has taken
over, the borrower has, in effect, obtained his
cash.

The remaining chapters are concerned with the
various problems and techniques currently relevant,
including type of issue, convertible, multiple
currency, and so forth; the most appropriate market, Luxembourg or elsewhere; and the particular
difficulties raised by particular countries and
borrowing centers.

NOTES TO CHAPTER 1

1. See Paul Einzig, "What Bankers Know, or
Ought to Know, About Foreign Exchange Theory,"
Quarterly Review (Banca Nazionale del Lavoro)
(September, 1964), p. 296.

2. Speech by Frank Manheim, "The European
Capital Market," Federal Trust Report, Special
Series No. 2 (London, 1967), p. 30.

3. Paul Einzig, Foreign Dollar Loans in Europe (London: Macmillan and Company, 1965), p. 26.

4. Ibid., p. 33, states: "The Chancellor of the Exchequer, Dr. Dalton, was openly hostile to international financing activities on ideological grounds. His attitude and that of his Government was characterized by a reply when pressed in Parliament to do something about the suspension of payments on the Japanese debt to British investors, to the effect that it served the British bondholders right to lose their money--why did they lend to Japan?"

5. Ibid., p. 42.

6. Robert Genillard, Federal Trust Report, op. cit., p. 30.

7. Claudio Segré, "Foreign Bond Issues in European Markets," Quarterly Review (Banca Nazionale del Lavoro) (March, 1964).

8. Figures from Federal Reserve System, "The Overseas Dollar Bond Market and Recent U.S. Borrowing Abroad," Staff Economic Studies, No. 22 (August, 1966); and "The Squeeze on Dollar Bonds," Economist (January 22, 1966).

9. The Chase Manhattan Bank, "Report on Western Europe," No. 40 (March-April, 1966).

10. For a general survey on European capital markets, see "Capital Markets in Europe," published by the economist research group of four major banks, March, 1965. For France in particular, see Michael Green, "Restoring Paris as a Financial Centre," The Banker (London) (December, 1966).

11. European Economic Community, The Development of a European Capital Market, Commission Report (November, 1966), Summary, Chapter 1.

2

TYPES OF BOND
ISSUES AND
USUAL FEATURES

This chapter will attempt to outline the major
decisions that have to be taken with regard to the
structure and form of an international bond issue
and the various alternatives open to the borrower.
Much use is made of historical examples with particular emphasis on recent trends. Emphasis is put
on the public company flotation rather than government or international institutional forms of flotation, with particular emphasis on U.S. subsidiaries
abroad.

LOCATION OF THE SUBSIDIARY

When a U.S. company wishes to raise money
abroad, the three major problems are the location
of the appropriate subsidiary, the currency of the
issue, and the form of the issue (that is, convertible, parallel, optional currency, and so forth).
We shall assume that the amount to be raised has
already been decided. The technical problems of
underwriting arrangements and selling will be discussed later, as will the cost of the loan in terms
of the appropriate interest rate or return on investment.

First, it is clear that a subsidiary must be
employed, for the whole point of the exercise is
to lighten the strain on the U.S. balance of payments. If the parent company is the borrower, and
U.S. investors are permitted to subscribe, the
balance-of-payments problem is not solved. Furthermore, the interest on the obligation would have

U.S. withholding tax of 30 per cent deducted at the
source--a matter of considerable dismay to some foreign investors--while stringent Security and Exchange Commission (SEC) requirements would have to
be fulfilled. The subsidiary, appropriately located, must provide freedom from any onerous withholding tax, must not cause any major capital outflow from the U.S., and must therefore be attractive to foreign investors. U.S. investors will be
subject to the interest-equalization tax on purchase, and U.S. nationals are not normally permitted
any participation in the initial placing. (Bonds
that are free from U.S. interest-equalization tax
are discussed later.)

In practice, the decision as to where the subsidiary should be is reduced to a choice between
the U.S. itself or Luxembourg. The latter country
is very popular because Luxembourg imposes no withholding tax on bond interest, and domestic taxes
are low (see Chapter 5). On the other hand, a U.S.
incorporated subsidiary is also free from withholding tax if over 80 per cent of its earnings come
from sources outside the U.S. And it will be treated
for the purposes of interest-equalization tax and
voluntary guidelines as if it were a nonresident
company.

Naturally, U.S. borrowers tend to prefer a
U.S. subsidiary; usually for convenience it is incorporated in Delaware,which has the most amenable
legislation for holding companies, while European
borrowers tend to prefer Luxembourg. An additional
point is the fact that U.S. tax law is considered
more stable than Luxembourg tax law, especially because the latter is already under attack from its
EEC partners, particularly France, for its relatively tax-free environment. Thus, it is not surprising that the Delaware corporations have come
out on the top of the list in recent issues.

Generally, the subsidiary will merely act as
a moneybox, "tapping European millions and passing
them on to other European subsidiaries."[1] Requirements for the underlying equity base will be

discussed in more detail later. Here it is sufficient to say that it is advisable to inject some
equity cash in order to provide a base, although it
may not be legally required. In fact, most subsidiaries are "rather heavily capitalized."[2] For example, the Pepsico Overseas Corporation prospectus
for the $30 million offering of 4-1/2 per cent con-
vertible debentures stated:

> . . . capital stock consists of 1,000
> shares of common stock par value $1.00
> per share. Prior to the issue of the
> debentures to the underwriters, the
> guarantor, i.e. Pepsico Inc., will
> purchase all of such stock for cash at
> $1,000 a share, or an aggregate cash
> consideration of $1,000,000. On, or
> prior to, June 1st 1966, the guarantor
> will make such contribution in cash,
> securities, or other property in order
> that the equity capital of the company
> will be no less than $6,000,000.[3]

Also note Pepsico Inc.'s comments on the purpose of the issue:

> The guarantor caused the Company to be
> formed for the principal purpose of
> obtaining funds for the capital re-
> quirements of the guarantor's inter-
> national operations. The Company in-
> tends to assist the U.S. Government's
> voluntary programme for improving the
> balance of payments position of the
> United States of America, by using the
> proceeds from the sale of the deben-
> tures, none of which is being offered
> in the U.S.A., its territories or its
> possessions, or to nationals or citi-
> zens thereof, or persons (including
> corporations) residing or normally
> residing therein, for acquiring inter-
> ests in foreign companies and for
> making investments in and loans to

foreign subsidiaries and affiliates and
other foreign companies in which the
guarantor directly or indirectly has or
shall have acquired an interest.[4]

CURRENCY OF THE ISSUE

Single-Currency Loans

When the location of the subsidiary is decided upon, the next and major problem is the decision regarding the currency of issue. If history
is any guide, the prime choice will be the dollar.
Table 4 gives relevant currency statistics since
1962, based on EEC data, and the dollar clearly
emerges as the favorite.

The principal reason for the popularity of the
dollar is its considerable current and (expected)
future strength, together with its worldwide
marketability. Allied to this is the strong growth
in overseas-held dollars, the prime position of the
U.S. in the political and economic world, and the
relative lack of its currency from any controls.
Some of these reasons are clearly interdependent,
and indeed some cause the dollar to have ever-
increasing importance. For example, note the following:

> . . . internationalisation of the
> dollar--powered on the short-term
> side by the Euro-dollar deposit
> market--has undoubtably facilitated
> the sale of U.S. corporate bonds in
> Europe. In turn, the appearance of
> these high-yielding long-term dollar
> obligations has increased the dollar's
> international usefulness, motivating
> more foreigners to hold more of their
> wealth in U.S. dollars. To the extent
> this represents a shift in foreigners'
> financial preferences, it strengthens
> the international position of the
> dollar.[5]

TABLE 4

Public International Bond Issues, 1962-66
(tabulated by currency in million-dollar equivalents)

Currency	Years in Amounts					Years in Percentages				
	1962	1963	1964	1965	1966	1962	1963	1964	1965	1966
U.S. Dollars	--	--	409.50[a]	550.5	842.5	--	--	--	--	--
U.S. Dollars	501.2	409.6	412.80[b]	490.0	343.0	65.5	51.5	62.2	62.0	60.5
U.C.	5.0	43.0	10.00	--	74.1	0.6	5.3	0.8	--	3.8
German DM	25.0	40.0	223.75	315.0	327.7	3.3	5.0	16.7	18.8	16.6
Swiss Francs	160.2	149.1	92.72	86.0	100.3	20.9	18.7	7.0	5.0	5.0
Belgian Francs	--	--	--	10.0	10.0	--	--	--	0.6	0.5
Dutch Guilders	39.3	--	15.43	57.5	--	5.1	--	1.1	3.4	--
French Francs	--	--	30.00	25.0	40.0	--	--	2.2	1.4	2.0
United Kingdom Pounds	5.6	130.9	133.60	101.2	145.6	0.7	16.4	10.0	6.0	7.3
Canadian Dollars	--	--	--	23.0	18.4	--	--	--	1.4	0.9
Italian Liras	24.0	24.0	--	24.0	67.2	3.1	3.1	--	1.4	3.4
Luxembourg Francs	6.0	--	--	0.6	--	0.8	--	--	--	--
Total	766.3	796.6	1,327.80	1,682.8	1,968.8	100.0	100.0	100.0	100.0	100.0

[a]U.S. dollar-denominated loans, subject to interest-equalization tax.

[b]Exempt issues.

Source: Banking Commission of the European Economic Community.

Second in importance to the dollar but a long
way behind it comes the West German Deutsche mark.
Du Pont employed this currency, as did Gulf Oil,
both raising 100 million DM ($25 million). German
currency is favored partly because of its strength
and partly because of the aid provided by the German authorities and the expertise of their major
banks. Indeed, the German authorities have no objection to the outflow of their funds in order to
purchase such issues, and DM bonds issued by a nonresident borrower are free from the 25 per cent
withholding tax imposed on nonresident owners of
domestic German bonds. In addition, the German DM
is one of the few world currencies that is relatively free from exchange control restrictions and
more or less freely convertible.

One objection that has been raised is that the
high domestic German interest-rate structure could
cause problems if domestic German investors ever
have to "take over" the load of the international
issue, that is, if foreign investors lose confidence in the DM.[6] But this is not an immediate
problem, and in the meantime, the DM remains attractive.

One currency that should have been attractive
is the Swiss franc. Its interest rates are among
the lowest in Europe, and the currency is unques-
tionably strong. However, Swiss authorities have
certainly not encouraged the franc's use, and they
claim that the monetary movements which might occur could disrupt their small economy. Furthermore, direct borrowing costs such as underwriting
are high, and there is a long waiting list. Finally, Swiss banks cannot underwrite international
issues without being subject to some measure of tax
discussed below.

One issue that did attempt to run the gaunt-
let for Swiss approval was the 60 million Swiss
franc issue of the city of Copenhagen in 1963. The
outcry was immediate. According to Hans Bär, of
Julius Bär and Company: "A syndicate of London
banks tried to initiate the scheme . . . without

any participation whatsoever on the part of Swiss banks, above all without the permission or rather over the objections of the Swiss National Bank."[7]

Whether or not the Swiss authorities are justified in their isolationist attitude remains to be seen. Possibly it will soon be almost impossible for a single economy to insulate itself against the increasing internationalization of finance, capital flows, and interest-rate differentials. Indeed, Robert Genillard, himself a Swiss, is quite out-spoken on the subject:

> Expressing a strictly personal view, I cannot help but feel that while isola-tion has served my country's financial interest well in the past and neutrality remains the foundation of its interna-tional existence, Switzerland as a liberal and international-minded country could play a most constructive role of enlightened self-interest by a more direct participation in international developments such as the Euro-bond market, while the economic consequences would seem in part to be unduly feared and in part are anyway inevitable.[8]

Apart from the dollar, the Swiss franc, and the Deutsche mark, seven other national currencies have been employed to a lesser extent. These are the Belgian franc, the Dutch florin, the French franc, the English pound, the Canadian dollar, the Italian lira, and the Luxembourg franc. But they have not made any significant impact on the inter-national bond scene for a variety of reasons, the principal one, of course, being the fear of de-valuation or revaluation.

However, one currency that may increase in importance in the years ahead is the French franc. Late in 1966, to a considerable extent the French authorities released their stranglehold on foreign-exchange control and international dealings in general, with the result that a considerable

number of French franc denominated international
bond issues are in the pipeline. Not only is the
franc one of the strongest of the European currencies, but a wealth of expertise also exists in Paris
to bring French currency to the forefront in international operations. Thus, with the low, internal
interest-rate structure, the franc appears certain
to make a major impact on the international scene,
always provided, of course, that the government
does not have a change of mind and trouble does not
arise with the EEC.

Over the past few years, considerable ingenuity
has been exercised by international bankers in the
attempt to broaden the currency base of international bond markets. The three principal techniques have been the optional currency or multicurrency loan, the parallel loan, and the unit-of-
account loan. Even though none of these techniques
has gained any measure of popularity, it is important to outline their development and analyze the
considerable problems they raise.

Optional-Currency Loans

The optional-currency loan is an obvious extension of the single-currency loan. The loan is
issued in a major currency (often sterling), but the
creditor has the right to request repayment of
interest and capital in one of several currencies
specified, at an exchange rate based on the parity
existing at the time of the issue. For example,
in 1964, the city of Turin raised £4 million in
London with payment optional in sterling or German
marks at a fixed rate of exchange; in the same year,
the Government of Finland raised DM40 million in
Germany with a repayment option in DM or U.S. dollars.

Naturally, the optional currency loan is extremely attractive to investors because they are
well protected against exchange risks. For the
same reason, such loans are unpopular as far as
borrowers are concerned, because a large additional

liability could arise should any one of the specified currencies be revalued (naturally all the
lenders will request repayment in this currency).
In addition, as Julius Bär points out, the ultimate
legality of a currency option that might be con-
strued as something akin to a gold clause, could
one day be challenged.[9]

Parallel Loans

An alternative to the multiple-currency loan
is the parallel loan proposed by Dr. Hermann Abs of
the Deutsche Bank. In this instance, the loan is
divided into batches and placed simultaneously on
different markets in the appropriate currency and
yield that appears to be dictated by local requirements. The ENEL issue (Italian Electricity Company) was the only major one and was made in the sum-
mer of 1965. Separate batches of this 15-year
6 per cent bond were issued in the six EEC countries, with prices varying from 95 (Germany, Hol-
land, and Luxembourg), through 95-1/2 (France) to
96 (Italy). However, despite the apparently sound
principle that investors would prefer to subscribe
in their own currency and thus total market ab-
sorbtion would be larger, the loan was not a success, and the parallel technique has not become
popular.

The main problem is the lack of uniformity in
national tax and other financial regulations in
major European countries. It is difficult to
synchronize various issues, and time-lags (anathema
to underwriters), are inevitable. Also, of course
the differing interest rates prevailing in the
several tranches could "unleash arbitrage operations which could literally endanger an entire
underwriting transaction,"[10] while a related problem is the tendency of subscriptions to accumulate
in the highest yielding tranche. Finally, the
currency problem is not really solved, as the whole
operation could be thrown into confusion by a speculative attack on one particular currency.

Unit-of-Account Loans

The most ambitious of all multicurrency proposals was the unit-of-account loan. A steady
trickle of these issues have been coming to the
market, the first being SACOR (Portugese Petroleum
Company) in February, 1961; one of the more recent
was CUF (Portugese Chemical Company) in December,
1966. The latter loan was issued at 99 and had
moved to 101-1/2 by the beginning of March, 1967.

The present value of the unit of account,
formerly used by the European Payments Union, is
defined in Article 26 of the organization's charter
as 0.88867088 grams of fine gold. In addition, the
unit of account is defined in terms of seventeen
reference currencies, and the gold value of a
reference currency at any time is its gold value
then current, as declared to and accepted by the
International Monetary Fund. (For a full definition, see Table 5.) The relation between the
present value of the unit of account and the present
gold values of the reference currencies is given in
Table 5. Note that because the unit of account is
based on gold, as are the seventeen reference
currencies (directly or indirectly), there must
exist a fixed proportion between each currency and
the unit of account.

It is important to emphasize that the unit of
account is not a means of exchange; it is solely an
artificial yardstick used to measure the value of
contractual loan obligations. Under the usual
definition, the unit of account changes in value
only if all the reference currencies change in value, and then only if two thirds of them have
changed in the same direction. If these conditions
were satisfied, the unit of account would be adjusted in the same direction and proportion as the
currency that among the two thirds had changed
least after a lapse of two years. The unit-of-
account borrower is free to choose the reference
currency in which he would like to receive the
loan, while the lender has the right to demand

payment of both principal and interest in the
reference currency of his choice.

What this complicated formula does in effect
is protect both the borrower and the lender from
most of the risks inherent in a normal currency
loan. For the lender, a devaluation of the reference currency will be irrelevant because he will
receive more of it in exact proportion to the devaluation, and a borrower is similarly protected in
the case of a revaluation. On the other hand, a
borrower is not covered if his own currency is devalued, nor is the lender if his currency is revalued.

Nevertheless, the formula is more attractive
to the debtor than a multicurrency clause. The
situation has been summarized thus:

> If there is a general revaluation, the
> obligations will, in the case of a
> multiple currency clause, vary in line
> with the currency which has been re-
> valued the most. In the case of the
> unit of account, however, the obliga-
> tions will vary in the same proportions
> as the currency which has been revalued
> the least. Moreover the obligation in
> units of account is much more stable,
> as it only changes after the seventeen
> currencies have been altered. In the
> case of the multiple currency clause,
> it is sufficient for one currency to
> change in order to cause the obligation
> to undergo an alteration. It may be
> said that in the case of the multiple
> currency clause, the debtor bears the
> risk of other currencies as well as
> that of his own currency; in the case
> of the unit of account, however, his
> obligations do not change as long as
> his own currency remains unchanged.[11]

TABLE 5

Unit-of-Account Issues, 1961-66

Company	Issue Date	Amount (in millions)	Term (in years)	Coupon	Issue Price	Recent Price (where available)
SACOR (Portugal)	Feb., 1961	5.0	17	5-3/4	99	--
SACOR (Portugal)	Mar., 1962	5.0	16	5-3/4	99	--
Norges Kommunal Bank	Jan., 1963	12.0	20	5-1/2	99	97
Imatran Voima (Finland)	July, 1963	5.0	15	6	97	94-3/4
Cassa per il mezzo Giorno (Italy)	Oct., 1963	16.0	15	5-1/2	99-1/4	94-3/4
Banco de Fomento Nacional (Portugal)	Nov., 1963	10.0	15	5-1/2	97-1/2	95
Assoc. Municipalities Copenhagen	Apr., 1964	10.0	20	5-5/8	98	94-1/2
ECSC	Jan., 1966	20.0	20	5-3/4	99-3/8	94-3/4
Redernes Skibskredit (Norway)	Feb., 1966	8.5	14	6	98	95-3/4
Mexican Electricity	Apr., 1966	20.0	20	6-1/2	97-1/2	92-1/2
Hojgaard & Schultz (Denmark)	Aug., 1966	4.6	7	6	96	--
SACOR (Portugal)	Oct., 1966	6.0	10	6-3/4	97	101-1/2
CUF (Portugal)	Dec., 1966	5.0	10	7	99	102-3/4
Copenhagen County Authority	Dec., 1966	10.0	10	6-3/4	98	101-1/4

DEFINITIONS OF A UNIT OF ACCOUNT

(Extracted from the Prospectus of the 5-3/4% C.E.C.A. 1966 Loan)

DEFINITIONS

a) Present Value of the Unit of Account:

The present value of the Unit of Account is that of the Unit of Account of the European Payments Union, now dissolved, as this value was defined in Article 26(a) of the charter of that organization, i.e., 0.88867088 grams of fine gold.

b) Reference Currencies:

The reference currencies mentioned herein are the currencies of the 17 member countries of the former European Payments Union, provided that any currency without a gold value as defined below (fluctuating currency) shall cease to be considered a reference currency until it shall have re-acquired a gold value.

c) Gold Values of the Reference Currencies:

The gold value of a reference currency, at any given time, is its gold value then current, as declared to and concurred in by the International Monetary Fund; or (in the absence of such a declaration and acceptance) as determined by the official definition given to the currency by the country of issue, either in terms of gold or by reference to another currency having a gold value.

The relation between the present value of the Unit of Account and the present gold value of the reference currencies is:

1 UA =   26.000   0 schilling (Austria)
1 UA =   50.000   0 franc (Belgium)
1 UA =   6.907   14 krone (Denmark)
1 UA =   4.937   06 franc (France)
1 UA =   4.000   00 mark (Federal Republic of Germany)
1 UA =   30.000   0 drachma (Greece)
1 UA =   43.000   0 krona (Iceland)
1 UA =   0.357 143 pound (Ireland)
1 UA =   625.000   lira (Italy)
1 UA =   50.000   0 franc (Luxembourg)
1 UA =   3.620   00 guilder (Netherlands)
1 UA =   7.142   86 krone (Norway)
1 UA =   28.750   0 escudo (Portugal)
1 UA =   5.173   21 krona (Sweden)
1 UA =   4.372   82 franc (Switzerland)
1 UA =   9.000   00 pound (Turkey)
1 UA =   0.357 143 pound sterling (United Kingdom)

Despite these manifold advantages, the unit of account has not proved popular, partly due to its considerable complexity, and partly due to political difficulties. For example, Switzerland has protested strongly against the use of the Swiss franc as a reference currency on internal interest-rate grounds, while the complicated rules of United Kingdom exchange control and the premium dollar market more or less exclude sterling. In addition, governments do not like any trends toward supranational finance. As J. C. Ingram said:

> . . . unit-of-account bonds constitute a partial step toward capital-market integration in Europe where national capital markets are and remain fragmented, a true haven for isolationists. Despite their many advantages, the prospects for unit-of-account bonds are not bright. With no clear political mandate for capital-market integration, central bank dislike of them probably means that they will continue to play a minor role in international finance.[12]

This was written in late 1964, and although the outlook for capital-market integration is somewhat brighter, the statement still remains broadly correct.

But a steady trickle of bonds still comes to the markets. U.S. companies have never used this route because the dollar has always remained a firm favorite, but they may consider it in the future.[13]

CONVERTIBLE LOANS

Thus far we have only considered straight loans. But the borrower in a major company can also issue convertible loans. Or, carrying sophistication one stage further, he can issue loans with warrants attached. The ultimate step (discussed in Chapter 7) of issuing equity has not yet been attempted.

The arguments for and against convertible issues are well known,[14] and it is sufficient at this stage to say that their main advantage is that they are cheaper; their main disadvantage is that they dilute the existing equity. In addition, rules of some countries, notably the United Kingdom (see Chapter 4), may place difficulties in the way of such issues. On the other hand, in a congested market they may prove a necessary "sweetener," and were employed as such by many U. S. corporations in 1966. Among the giants who used this route were Pepsico, Federated Department Stores, W. R. Grace, General Electric, and Monsanto. Interest rates were generally 1-1/2 per cent lower than the equivalent straight issue, while conversion premiums into common stock of the parent-issuing company ranged to 15 per cent, with conversion rights normally running from twelve to eighteen months after the original issue for redemption.

For example, on February 16, 1966, Pepsico Overseas Corporation offered $30 million of 4-1/2 per cent guaranteed-convertible debentures, due in 1981. The prospectus stated: "The debentures will be convertible at their principal amount by exchange for Capital Stock of the Guarantor at any time on or after September 1, 1967, and on or prior to February 26, 1981, at the conversion price of $93 per share." Since the shares of Pepsico were then $81-1/2, the premium was approximately 15 per cent. The bonds were offered at 100, and had moved ahead to 104 by March, 1967. By mid-August, 1967, they stood at 110.

One of the most interesting convertible issues was a $30 million offering in February, 1966, by two subsidiaries of International Telephone and Telegraph Corporation. One subsidiary offered $15 million of 6 per cent 20-year sinking-fund debentures, while the other offered $15 million of

20-year, 4-1/2 per cent convertible debentures.
The bonds were then offered as a "package," thus
combining "the advantages of cost-cutting that the
convertible debentures carry with the non-equity-
diluting advantages of the non-convertible sinking-
fund bond."[15]

WARRANT ISSUES

The bonds were offered in $1,000 units, con-
sisting of $500 in the principal amount of each is-
sue of debenture, at 97-1/2. The conversion price
into International Telephone and Telegraph was
$82. By March, 1967, with I.T.&T. quoted at $89,
the 4-1/2 per cent bonds stood at 111-1/2 and the
6 per cent bonds at 100, so the issue proved to be
a success.

A further extension of convertibility is to
the bond-carrying warrants giving the right to
subscribe for shares at a predetermined price.
These warrants are usually detachable and have an
independent quotation. The essential difference
between this form of issue and the convertible has
been summarized thus: "The convertible buyer wants
reasonable security with some equity participation,
while the purchaser of warrants wants a highly-
geared means of taking a view on the share price of
a particular company."[16] The issue of bonds with
warrants is normally more expensive than a convertible issue but can often provide a useful
sweetener to make an issue "go." In essence, warrants are long-term options and tend to appeal to
the more speculative investor.

Two major warrant issues recently have both
been on behalf of Italian companies. One was by
Instituto per la Ricostruzione Industriale (IRI),
and the other and more interesting, by Societa
Generale Immobiliare (SGI). This was a complicated but successful issue involving two different
warrants. The prospectus states:

> There will be issued, attached to
> each Bond, two detachable bearer
> warrants designated as warrant A and
> warrant B. . . . Warrant A will en-
> title the bearer to purchase, not
> later than December 31, 1970, 250
> shares of lire 250 each fully paid of
> the Guarantor for U.S. $230 [equiva-
> lent at the present mean International
> Monetary Fund (IMF) exchange rate to
> lire 575 per share] payable in cash.
> Warrant B will entitle the bearer to
> purchase not later than June 30, 1975,
> 250 shares of lire 250 each fully paid
> of the guarantor for U.S. $250 [625 lire
> per share] payable in cash or, in the
> case of surrender by any bearer of four
> or more B warrants and so long as any
> bonds are outstanding, by tendering a
> bond or bonds in satisfaction of an
> amount equivalent to the nominal amount
> of the bonds tendered.

By mid-March, 1967, the SGI bonds (cum warrants)
were quoted at 104-1/4 and the warrants at 2-1/4
each. SGI common shares were quoted on the Milan
Stock Exchange at lire 490.

It does appear surprising that no U.S. borrowers to date have attempted this form of issue.
While it is true that warrant-bonds are a half-way-
home between the straight bond and the convertible,
and to some extent incur the disadvantages of both
(that is, high cost and equity dilution), they
would appear to be attractive to the less solidly
based concern where the possibilities both of
capital appreciation and loss are high. To the
investor in warrants, capital appreciation remains,
and the cost is limited; to the company, the over-
all interest cost is diminished to the extent that
the warrants are valued by the investor.

Moreover, this form of issue is not uncommon
in the U.S.; it is unknown in many other countries,

including the United Kingdom, and they have every
reason for holding to the more conventional routes.
A further major advantage to the U.S. company operating abroad is that the U.S. investor will only
pay the interest-equalization tax on the price of
the warrant (if he buys the detachable warrant) instead of on the entire convertible bond. So the
U.S. investor may be encouraged to invest in these
instruments despite the tax. If they convert, of
course, the tax on the entire conversion amount
will no doubt become payable; but there is nothing
to stop them from selling the warrants at a hand-
some profit if the underlying share price goes up.

TIME-GUARANTEED NOTES

So far, we have only considered medium-term
international bonds, with maturities in the range
of 15 to 20 years. However, in 1966, a new phenomenon, inspired by the high interest-rate structure
and general congestion, made an appearance, the
five-year guaranteed note. Continental Oil International Finance Corporation, a subsidiary of
Continental Oil Company, was the first in the field,
in May, 1966. Subsequently, many others have followed, including Cabot, Goodyear, Hercules, and
Marathon from the U.S., and Ameribas and
Osterreichische Investionskredit from Europe.

This form of financing is designed to appeal
to a broader strata of investors, while ensuring
that high interest rate costs do not become a drag
on the company over a long period. To date, they
have had a remarkable success. In principle, they
exhibit the same characteristics of the long-term
loan, with similar provisions as to guarantee, payment of principal and interest, optional redemption (usually at par), and various future taxation
safeguards. As of mid-September, 1967, most issues of this type stood at a premium (owing of
course to the recent downward trend in Euro-dollar
rates).

The problems facing a company considering this
form of issue are quite different from the problem
of whether or not to raise long-term finance via the
international bond market. In the latter case, a
bond issue may be the only possibility (especially
if available retained earnings are small); in the
former and shorter-term case, many alternatives are
available. For example, the company could resort to
direct Euro-dollar borrowing, to multicurrency
credit lines or to direct bank borrowing (including
medium-term bank loans).[17]

Two recent interesting innovations arising
from the continuously increasing sophistication of
Euro-dollar markets are the two-year revolving
credit line and the rise of the Euro-dollar in the
U.S. The former method, which involves the opening
of several-year, long credits on a ninety-day basis
has been employed by IBM and Pfizer.[18] The interest
rate is fixed every ninety days on drawing or re-
newal, so there is little chance of any distortion
in rates. The latter method was employed by Ling-
Temco-Vought to finance a large acquisition. A
two-year Euro-dollar loan from sixteen non-U.S.
banks was negotiated.[19]

Because the attractions and difficulties of
these alternatives are outside the scope of this
book, it is sufficient to note that difficulties do
exist, among them what J. S. G. Wilson calls the
"shifting temporal gap"[20] and the corporation financial executives need to have considerable knowledge
of the conditions prevailing in various countries.
For example, they should know that borrowing for up
to two years is relatively easy and cheap in
Switzerland, while long-term bond issues are extremely difficult.

As far as the bond investor in general is concerned, five-year notes are a logical extension to
an integrated bond market. Indeed, as mentioned
in Chapter 1, the whole of international finance
has become time-integrated in recent years, with
Euro-dollars available at the short end and

long-term bonds at the long end. As more issues
come to the market, the more will integration proceed as secondary dealings develop.

USUAL FEATURES AND GUARANTEES

Now that we have considered the general aspects of location of the subsidiary, currency, type,
and length of loan, we can proceed to a more detailed consideration of the usual features and
guarantees involved in international-bond financing.

As indicated earlier, the bonds will usually
be issued via a Luxembourg or Delaware subsidiary,
incorporated for the purpose of obtaining funds for
investment in foreign subsidiaries and affiliates.
For example, early in 1966, Avon Products Incorporated, the world's largest manufacturer and dis-
tributor of cosmetics and toiletries, raised
$15 million via Avon Overseas Capital Corporation.
The latter company was in fact incorporated in New
York, but (in accordance with earlier remarks) the
prospectus states:

> Avon Overseas contemplates conducting
> its business so that more than 80% of
> its gross income will be derived from
> sources outside the United States in
> order that payments on the Bonds to
> holders who are foreign corporations,
> non-resident alien individuals, non-
> resident alien fiduciaries and non-
> resident foreign partnerships will not
> be subject to United States income
> taxes.
> . . . Avon Overseas was formed by
> Avon to obtain funds from sources other
> than citizens or residents of the
> United States to be used to meet the
> financial requirements of Avon's
> foreign subsidiaries, in keeping with
> the Government's voluntary programme
> for improving the balance-of-payments
> position of the United States.

The latter sentence is standard. For example, the Beecham International Holdings prospectus for the $15 million issue in 1966 in a similar vein states: "The Company was incorporated in the Grand Duchy of Luxembourg . . . for the purpose of making investments in and financing the capital requirements of subsidiary companies of Beecham located outside the United Kingdom." Naturally Beecham was not concerned with the U.S. balance-of-payments position.

The debentures are usually unsecured obligations of the subsidiary, but they are always guaranteed by the parent company. The statement that usually appears in the prospectus is as follows: The guarantor will unconditionally guarantee the due and punctual payment of the principal, premium if any, interest, and sinking fund on the debentures when and as the same shall become due and payable. In some European cases, where the borrower is the major company, the issue will be government guaranteed. Thus the $9 million issue by Aktiebolaget Gotaverken, a leading shipbuilding company, was unconditionally guaranteed by the Kingdom of Sweden; and the $15 million Austrian Electricity Loan was unconditionally guaranteed by the Republic of Austria.

As mentioned earlier, the subsidiary company must provide some form of equity base for the borrowing despite the parent guarantee. This requirement is partly a reflection of local laws (see Chapter 3), and it is interpreted in various ways by various companies. For example, Phillips Petroleum was generous, providing a $6 million base for the $25 million issue via Phillips Petroleum International Investment, and Bristol-Myers provided $3 million for the $15 million issue by their subsidiary. However the more recent trend appears to be toward a so-called thinner capitalization of the subsidiary, and debt-to-equity ratios of 10 to 1 are not uncommon. For example, Ameribas Holdings S.A., made a five-year $15 million issue in 1966 with an underlying equity of only $1.5 million.

Sinking Funds

Sinking-fund provisions are fairly universal
for straight bond issues by companies and may or
may not appear in convertible issues. In the case
of U.S. companies, the usual rule is that sufficient cash is paid to the trustee over a period of
years to redeem about 90 per cent of the principal
amount of debentures (which, of course, accumulated,
should ensure entire repayment. In fact, it is
simple to show that the accumulation rate assumed
in the case of a ten-year 90 per cent sinking fund
is less than 2-1/2 per cent per year; thus, the
terms are eminently reasonable. Sometimes the
percentage is higher (International Standard Electric 6 per cent debentures have a figure of 96 per
cent) but the following clause is fairly typical.
It is taken from the Amax Holdings Incorporated
prospectus, dated May 24, 1967, for the issue of
$25 million, 6-1/4 per cent guaranteed sinking-
fund debentures, due in 1982.

> The debentures will be subject to re-
> demption through a sinking fund on
> June 1, 1972 and on each June 1 there-
> after to and including June 1, 1981,
> on at least 30 days' notice, at the
> principal amount thereof together with
> accrued interest thereon. As a sinking
> fund for such redemption Holdings will
> pay to the paying agent in New York City
> sums sufficient to redeem, on each of
> the above redemption dates, $2,200,000
> principal amount of debentures. Hold-
> ings may reduce any sinking-fund payment
> by delivering for credit against such
> sinking-fund payment, at their principal
> amounts, debentures redeemed or other-
> wise acquired by Holdings or Amax.

In some issues (such as Avon Overseas), an
additional optional sinking fund--any installment
of which never exceeds the amount of the mandatory
sinking-fund payment--is established. Convertible

issues such as Clark Equipment Overseas possess
sinking funds, and others such as Pepsico Overseas
do not. Where such sinking funds exist, they
normally only provide for about 50 per cent of the
total issue. For example, the ISE Finance convertible issue has a sinking fund providing for the
redemption of 45 per cent of the issue; but, as
mentioned above, the ISE debenture provides for
96 per cent of its issue.

The redemption of European issues is complicated by the fact that such issues as European
Investment Bank at 6-1/2 per cent in 1986 are redeemable by installments. In such cases, the bonds
are usually redeemable at par in specified quantities at specified dates either through drawings by
lot, or by open-market purchases by the company or
both. In the latter case, the bonds so purchased
can be set against the redemption requirements (at
par), and sometimes limitations apply. For example,
the Austrian Electricity Loan "may at any time
purchase bonds in the open market at any price or
by private treaty at a price not exceeding 105 per
cent." The De Beers issue of April, 1967, had a
similar provision, while the National Lead Overseas
Corporation, May, 1967 issue, must "purchase in the
market bonds . . . if and in so far as such purchases are possible at market prices below par."
The situation is summed up by the following quotation from the Siemens Europa DM 100 million issue.

> The borrower will open a sinking fund
> in its name during the life of the
> issue. . . . The sinking-fund agent
> is obliged to purchase bonds in the
> market for the sinking fund if the
> bonds are officially quoted on the
> Frankfurt Stock Exchange below 100%.
> On this assumption, in each of the
> periods beginning August 1 and ending
> July 31 of the following year, bonds
> are to be purchased up to the amount
> of the annual installment falling due
> one each following November 1.

Notwithstanding the above obligations, the borrower is entitled to
purchase bonds at any time in the
open market or otherwise and, at its
option, to credit such bonds to the
sinking fund. . . . Insofar as the
bonds required for an annual installment are not provided out of the sinking fund, as many bonds as are necessary to cover the amount of the particular annual installment are to be
drawn by lot for this purpose.

Short-term bonds do not carry sinking funds.

Optional Redemption

An optional redemption clause, providing that
the company may redeem bonds prior to their contractual redemption date, is common. Naturally, a
premium is offered for this concession, usually
commencing at around 4-1/2 per cent, three to six
years after the issue, and falling by 1/2 per cent
per annum thereafter. An initial period within
which the bonds may not be redeemed is always provided, and the European installment issues also
provide for optional early redemption, although the
premium in this case is usually lower.

At this stage, the prospectus often contains
a major qualification to the so-called optional redemption clause. This safeguards the company
against any future tax changes in the countries
concerned and usually states the following: "Notwithstanding the foregoing if, as the result of
any change in, or amendment to, the laws of X affecting taxation . . . it is determined by the
company that it would be required to pay additional
interest . . ., then the company may, at its option,
redeem the bonds in whole at any time prior
to . . . upon not less than 30 days' notice." This
is a major modification safeguarding the company,
and provides, in effect, that the bonds can be redeemed at any time if there are any significant tax

changes; it arises from the various taxation
guarantees that must be provided.

Not all companies have this safeguard and, of
those that have, careful searching of the prospectus is often necessary. For example, the Siemens
Europa issue, referred to above, makes no qualification to its prepayment clause (which commences
November 1, 1972, at 102 per cent). But, later, in
the taxation clause it is stated: "In the event
that any such aforesaid taxes or duties should be
levied by means of deduction at source, the borrower may, on giving not less than 90 days' notice,
redeem all outstanding bonds on any interest payment date prior to November 1, 1972, at the price
of 104%."

Some companies, while omitting this obvious
safeguard, have provided extra safeguards to the
shareholders. For example, the Marathon International issue states that the convertible debentures may not be redeemed prior to a certain date
"unless the market price, as defined, for the
Common Stock of the Guarantor on each full business day within the 30 days preceding the fifteenth
day prior to the day upon which notice of redemption is first published is at least 135% of the
conversion price in effect on the day on which such
notice is first published."

Tax Provisions

The provisions regarding present and future
taxes are vital, and in most cases, they appear to
be adequate. Companies appear to be quite happy to
guarantee interest and principal "without withholding or deduction for or on account of any
present or future income tax (including any here-
after enacted)." In other words, the company
normally contracts to pay any future taxes itself,
so that the holder receives the amount he expected
to receive. This, of course, is subject to an
early redemption clause (discussed above). More
precisely, a standard example is provided by the

$5 million issue by SGI International Holdings S.A. guaranteed by Societa Generale Immobiliare.

> All payments of principal, premium (if any) and interest will be made without deduction of or on account of any present or future taxes or duties of whatsoever nature imposed or levied by or on behalf of the Grand Duchy of Luxembourg and, in the event of any such payment being made by the Guarantor, the Republic of Italy, or by or on behalf of any municipality or other political sub-division or taxing authority therein or thereof; and if any such taxes or duties shall at any time be imposed or levied, the Company or the Guarantor as the case may be will pay such amounts as may be necessary in respect of principal, premium (if any) and interest in order that the net amounts paid shall equal the respective amounts stated on the bonds and coupons. This provision will not affect the liability to Luxembourg taxes of persons otherwise subject to taxation in Luxembourg or to Italian taxes of persons otherwise subject to taxation in Italy.

However, while tax provisions are fairly adequate, exchange-control provisions are not always satisfactory. The latter arise when the borrowing entity contracts to repay currency that is not his domestic currency (or, if it is, a currency that is subject to local government exchange-control restrictions). The problem, of course, does not really arise with U.S. companies because the dollar is more or less free from restriction; but it does arise when so-called third countries borrow in dollars.

Einzig[21] has some strong words to say on the subject. He points out that any clause which depends on regulations now in force can easily be

blocked by future government legislation. The issues for the Instituto per la Ricostruzione
Industriale, a corporation owned by the Italian
Government, contain a similarly inadequate clause
that does not prevent the government from blocking
the transfer of interest and principal by simply
changing the law. On the other hand, as Einzig
also points out, some countries, notably Portugal,
Austria, and Sweden provide effective guarantees.
For example, the Austrian Brenner Autobahn issue
states: "The company has delivered to the trustee
a written undertaking by the National Bank of
Austria to permit the free transfer of funds
necessary for the payment of interest and the reim-
bursement of principal." Even more explicitly, the
Swedish Gotaverken issue states:

> Sveriges Riksbank has given its
> written approval for the issue of the
> Debentures. Such bank has also
> given an authorisation irrevocable by
> its terms, pursuant to which
> Gotaverken (and Sweden under the
> guarantee) may purchase in exchange
> for Swedish Kroner sufficient freely
> transferable United States dollars
> to pay principal, premium, if any,
> and interest on the Debentures in ac-
> cordance with their terms.

Nonetheless, some issues provide inadequate
exchange-control safeguards, and few approach this
ideal, cited by Einzig, from a Portuguese Government loan:

> The Republic of Portugal undertakes to
> transfer or make available all funds
> required for the service of the
> Bonds . . . in U.S. dollars under all
> circumstances without any limitations
> and outside any bilateral or multi-
> lateral payments or clearing agreement
> to which the Republic of Portugal may
> be a party at the times these payments
> are made.

United Kingdom exchange control is noted for its complexity, ad hoc administration, and rapid changes; in addition, the dislike of the Labour Government for overseas private investment is well known. One may therefore question the adequacy of the following, which heads the Beecham International Prospectus: "Approval of the Bank of England to the giving by Beecham of the guarantee of the Debentures has been obtained. The Company and Beecham have also obtained all other necessary consents and per- missions of the U.K. Treasury and the Bank of Eng- land for the issue of the Debentures and the issue of Ordinary Shares of Beecham on conversion." This is all very well but does not really preclude the government from blocking repayment if the guarantee were called by subsequent legislation. What are the so-called necessary consents? If they are as ad hoc as usual, a foreign holder should take care.

Currency Devaluation

In addition to the major provisions and guaran- tees usually required in an international bond as outlined above, "default" must be defined, with appropriate action indicated, and the usual inden- ture modifications allowed if two thirds of the debenture holders agree. Conversion rights, where applicable, are fairly standard (as stated earlier), but it is worthwhile to note that, depending on the terms of conversion, a holder may or may not benefit from a devaluation of the currency in which the underlying shares are denominated. For example, the conversion price of Beecham International is 32 shillings per share "except that the number of shares so issued will not exceed 223.2144 per $1,000 Debenture." This implies an exchange rate of $2.80 to the £1, and at first glance a holder would not gain by a sterling devaluation. However, a closer examination of the prospectus reveals that:

> To the extent that . . . the sum of
> the value of the maximum whole number
> of ordinary shares of Beecham computed

> at the then current conversion
> price . . . converted into dollars
> at the mean IMF exchange rate ruling
> on the date of conversion, is less
> than $1,000, such debenture shall
> not be converted . . . and shall
> bear interest at 6-1/4% p.a.

In other words, a holder will not lose by a devaluation, although his conversion rights are restricted, as they must be, or Beecham would have incurred an open-ended commitment on their issued ordinary capital. On the other hand, the SGI warrants state a conversion price in U.S. dollars; so a devaluation of the lire will not help the holder. In the SGI case, therefore, a devaluation raises the conversion price and protects the borrower. On the other hand, it is significant that the lender sometimes loses if the conversion currency is revalued. For example, taking Beecham again, if the pound were revalued so that $5 = £1, under the previous parity, the bondholder would obtain 223.2144 shares at the conversion price; at the revaluation, however, he will only obtain 125 shares, and the lender is not protected. On the other hand, a revaluation of the lire would benefit the SGI bondholder, because his conversion price would be effectively lowered.

EXPLANATORY TABULAR INFORMATION

In conclusion, the reader is referred to Table 12 (Statistical Appendix), which provides detailed statistics on all international bonds issued since the beginning of 1965. The various columns are self-explanatory. Note, in particular, that some issues are exempt from U.S. interest-equalization tax, for example, International Bank issues and Jamaican Government issues, and these are indicated by a check in the appropriate column. Total figures are provided for the years 1962-64 inclusive for comparison purposes.

The statistics have been compiled from many
sources, including the private files of leading
issuing houses, but the major source has been the
Banking Commission of the European Economic Community which keeps very detailed figures on this
market. Tables 6 and 7 provide a breakdown of the
statistics in Table 12 (Statistical Appendix), into
types of issue, and nationality of lender respectively.

The method of presenting international-bond
statistics is a controversial subject; and further,
almost endless permutations of the basis figures
can be constructed. Table 12 attempts to provide
all the facts, so that readers with different
purposes in mind can extract their own figures.
For example, certain issues included may not be
regarded as true international issues, but with the
aid of Table 12, they can easily be excluded from
the over-all totals.

Indeed, as mentioned in Chapter 1, the main
source of dissention is the definition of an international issue; and very little effort has been
made to distinguish between international and
national foreign issues. Table 12 provides all
issues that could possibly be described as international and to fill the above gap, Table 11 is also
included; this is a summary by White, Weld of what
they consider the international issues. Indeed, at
first sight, the discrepancies are surprising. For
example, the 1965 figure in Table 12 is $1,682.8
million, compared with the White, Weld figure of
$1,201. However, when IBRD (World Bank) issues
totaling $300 million equivalent, Commonwealth
issues in the United Kingdom totaling $37 million,
and Canadian issues in the U.S. totaling $100 mil-
lion are deducted, the discrepancy is reduced to
$44 million. This can be accounted for by such
difficulties of classification in issues as Unilever NV at 100 million florins ($28 million),
which appears to be a domestic issue but was internationally syndicated, and Eurofima at 40 million Swiss francs, which the Swiss consider a

TABLE 6

Classification by Types of Issue, 1962-66

	Equivalent (in millions of dollars)					Percentages				
	1962	1963	1964	1965	1966	1962	1963	1964	1965	1966
International Organizations	293.0	43.5	346.0	444.8	297.6	38.5	5.7	25.7	26.3	14.7
Governments and Public Bodies[a]	264.4	469.5	622.0	430.0	356.1	34.2	58.9	47.0	25.6	18.2
U.S. Industrial and Commercial	13.6	--	--	307.3	630.9	2.0	--	--	18.3	32.5
Non-U.S. Industrial and Commercial[b]	195.3	283.6	359.8	500.7	684.2	25.3	35.4	27.3	29.8	34.6
Total	766.3	796.6	1,327.8	1,682.8	1,968.8	100.0	100.0	100.0	100.0	100.0

[a]Includes only government and municipal issues.

[b]Includes semi-public issues.

51

TABLE 7

Classification by Nationality of Issuer, 1962-66

	Equivalent (in millions of dollars)			
	1962	1963	1964	1965
United States	13.6			307.3
Canada	2.3	25.0		100.0
Latin America		25.0	68.0	42.5
Europe	184.8	350.5	561.4	541.4
(Scandinavia)	(55.6)	(161.6)	(359.2)	(250.0)
(United Kingdom)	(44.2)	(4.5)	(14.7)	(48.0)
(EEC Member Countries)	(68.7)	(147.4)	(89.0)	(202.4)
(Others)	(16.3)	(37.0)	(98.5)	(41.0)
Asia	151.2	205.6	297.2	127.5
(Japan)	(91.0)	(139.0)	(198.4)	(87.5)
Commonwealth	121.4	147.0	55.2	119.3
(Australia and New Zealand)	(110.0)	(119.6)	(42.0)	(98.0)
International Organiza- tions	293.0	43.5	346.0	444.8
(EEC)	(84.0)	(39.0)	(145.5)	(114.0)
Total	766.3	796.6	1,327.8	1,682.8

1966	Percentages				
	1962	1963	1964	1965	1966
630.9	2.0			18.3	32.5
248.4		3.1		6.0	12.6
51.0		3.1	5.1	2.5	2.5
616.4	24.0	44.0	42.5	32.2	31.4
(101.2)	(7.2)	(20.2)	(27.0)	(14.8)	(5.2)
(51.4)	(5.8)	(0.6)	(1.1)	(2.8)	(2.6)
(232.6)	(9.0)	(18.5)	(6.7)	(12.0)	(11.8)
(231.2)	(2.0)	(4.7)	(7.7)	(2.6)	(11.8)
	19.5	25.6	22.5	7.6	
	(12.0)	(17.5)	(6.5)	(5.2)	
124.5	16.0	18.5	4.2	7.1	6.3
(83.6)	(14.5)	(15.0)	(3.2)	(5.8)	(4.2)
297.6	38.5	5.7	25.7	26.3	14.7
(199.0)	(11.0)	(4.9)	(11.0)	(6.8)	(10.0)
1,968.8	100.0	100.0	100.0	100.0	100.0

domestic issue although it is an international
organization. Note column four of the table which
provides total figures for what White, Weld consider internationally syndicated issues. It will
be apparent that three of the criteria for a truly
international issue are the composition of the issuing syndicate, the number and location of stock-
exchange listings, and the number and location of
paying agents. These subjects will all be discussed in Chapter 3.

Tables 6, 7, and 12 provide ample evidence
in statistical form for the major conclusions drawn
so far. The dominance of the dollar is evident, as
is the sudden recent volume of U.S. subsidiary
financing abroad. The recent introduction of short-
term issues is evident from the 1966 figures, while
various national trends, such as the decline of
Japanese financing, can be seen in Table 7.

The cost of raising finance will be discussed
more fully later. However, it should already be
apparent at this stage that international-bond
financing, while raising several unique complications, is by no means beyond the orbit of the
corporate financial department. Indeed, as we
have seen, most of the clauses are standard, and
the decisions with regard to location of the subsidiary, currency, and type of issue are by no
means insuperable. What we now have to consider
is the structure of the actual marketing operation,
taking into account the so-called incomprehensibil-
ity of non-U.S. markets.

NOTES TO CHAPTER 2

1. John Chown and Robert Valentine, "Tapping Europe's Millions," Management Today (July-August, 1966).

2. "How to Raise Long-Term Funds in the Tightening World Capital Market," Business International (November 5, 1965), which points out that Monsanto's equity for its $25 million issue in 1965 was $10 million.

3. Pepsico Overseas Corporation, Prospectus (February 16, 1966), p. 8.

4. Ibid.

5. The Chase Manhattan Bank, "Report on Western Europe," No. 40 (March-April, 1966).

6. For details, see "The European Capital Market," Federal Trust Report, Special Series No. 2, 1967, p. 38.

7. Hans Bär, "Bulletin" (Julius Bär and Co.), No. 13 (April, 1966).

8. Robert Genillard in "The European Capital Market," op. cit., p. 37.

9. Hans Bär, op. cit., p.3.

10. Ibid.

11. W. J. Hopper, "A Turntable for Capital" (Bow Group) (April, 1964), p. 66.

12. J. C. Ingram, "Unit-of-Account Bonds, Their Meaning and Function," Moorgate and Wall Street (Autumn, 1964).

13. The subject may be simplified by reading some of the numerous European articles available.

One of the best is J. C. Ingram, op. cit., as well as W. J. Hopper, op. cit., Appendix B; and Why Subscribe to Unit-of-Account Loans (Paris, Credit Commercial de France, 1966). Paul Einzig, in Foreign Dollar Loans in Europe (London: MacMillan and Co., 1965), discusses this subject in Chapter 11; a study of an actual unit-of-account prospectus also helpful is the Companhia Uniao Fabril (CUF) issue, pp. 6-7.

14. See, for example, Defosse, Les Obligations Convertibles en Action, Presses Universitaires de France.

15. Federal Reserve System, Staff Economic Studies, No. 22 (August, 1966), p. 24.

16. Chown and Valentine, op. cit.

17. "The Continuing Quest for International Funds: Alternatives to the Dollar-Bond Route," Business International (December 3, 1965).

18. For details, see Jonathon Radice, "Unwrapping the Enigma of the Euro-Markets," Financial Times (United Kingdom), December 5, 1966, p. 10.

19. "Euro-dollars--Growing Pool of International Money," Business International (March 10, 1967).

20. J.S. G. Wilson, "Some Aspects of the Development of Capital Markets," Quarterly Review (Banca Nazionale de Lavoro) (December, 1966), p. 263.

21. Paul Einzig, Foreign Dollar Loans in Europe (London: MacMillan and Company, 1965), pp. 54-55.

CHAPTER **3** RAISING FINANCE
ON THE INTERNATIONAL
BOND MARKET

We will now consider the structure of the
holding company which, as already indicated, is
usually necessary for the issue of international
bonds. Described in detail is the Luxembourg procedure as well as the general Luxembourg and European background of company law and taxation. We
hope that this will enable U.S. and other non-
European issuers to "comprehend the incomprehensi-
ble." Also discussed in this chapter are the marketing aspects of an international loan, prospectus
requirements, problems of stock-exchange listings,
underwriting and sales procedure, paying agents,
and delivery, as well as the history and present
state of secondary markets. The importance of secondary markets is obvious,[1] but little attempt to
date has been made to explain their somewhat eso-
teric mode of operation in the international bond
market, and we hope to fill this gap.

Now that we have considered the supply of the
market, we will analyze demand. The problem is
complicated, because demand statistics are almost
nonexistent, and large investment houses operating
in the field are naturally reluctant to disclose
anything which might prejudice their own or their
clients' interests. However, some interesting
general conclusions can be drawn, and various
trends can be identified.

Until this stage, most of our material has
been narrative rather than critical; however, more

critical comments will now become apparent and will gather force as we progress. In particular, much is wrong with present underwriting and secondary-market techniques, and the impact of the international bond market on the domestic and capital markets of the various countries involved must be seriously considered, with complaints already having been made by Germany and Switzerland.

THE PURE HOLDING COMPANY

As indicated in Chapter 2 and Table 12, holding-company operations have been mainly confined to the U.S. or Luxembourg. The former location has obvious benefits of convenience to U.S. companies, and in addition, if 80 per cent of the company's gross income is derived from sources outside the U.S., the company will be treated for purposes of interest-equalization tax, withholding tax, and voluntary guidelines as if it were a non-resident company. Thus, for example, in a Delaware prospectus the following sentence is usual: "The company contemplates conducting its business so that more than 80 per cent of its gross income will be derived from sources outside the United States of America." On the assumption that the U.S. technique is already at least somewhat familiar to the reader, the following discussion will deal with holding companies in Luxembourg.

A holding company, as defined in Article I of the Luxembourg Law of July 31, 1929, is:

> any Luxembourg company having as its sole object the taking of participating interests, in whatsoever form, in other Luxembourg or foreign undertakings, and the administration and development of such participating interests, so however that the company shall carry on no industrial activity nor maintain a commercial establishment open to the public.

There is a basic distinction between a pure holding
company and a mixed holding company; the former can
hold only shares in other companies, while the latter can engage in direct industrial or commercial
activity. We are concerned here with pure holding
companies which (as outlined above), must have as
their exclusive object the participation in other
companies or the management or administration of
these participations. In particular, the pure
holding company cannot own real estate; but it can
issue shares or bonds, and it can have liabilities
to outside parties.

THE DEBT-TO-EQUITY RATIO

The permitted ratio between debt and equity
does not appear to be clearly defined. One leading
Luxembourg bank states:

> Generally speaking, the revenue au-
> thorities aim to prevent any manifest
> disproportion between the amount of
> the capital and the amount due to
> creditors. Generally, they consider
> as out of proportion liabilities ex-
> ceeding three or four times the nom-
> inal capital of the company.[2]

However, as we have seen earlier, the recent trend
has been toward a thinner capitalization up to a
ratio of 10 to 1.

In the U.S., the situation with debt-to-equity
ratios is broadly similar. Originally, Delaware
corporations could more or less issue as much debt
as they wanted, but in the early months of 1966,
the U.S. Treasury began to compel firms to put
"substance" in their subsidiaries, by imposing an
upper limit of 5 to 1 on the ratio. Compliance
with this rule can be achieved either by injecting
cash (and subsequently investing it abroad), or
transferring the ownership of foreign subsidiaries
from overseas companies to the Delaware subsidiary.

As <u>Business International</u> points out,[3] the latter
course of action could result in a considerable
liability to U.S. capital-gains tax.

The 1929 law is also fairly broad in its field
of application:

> While the law of July 31, 1929, speaks
> only of "Holding Companies" the Luxem-
> bourg legislative intention does not
> confine it to Holding Companies proper,
> but applies it also to "financial par-
> ticipation companies" of various descrip-
> tions, such as controlling companies,
> investment trusts, finance companies
> and others.[4]

It is clear, therefore, that the holding companies come under the aegis of the Luxembourg law.
But just because a law exists is no reason that
companies should use it. In fact, Luxembourg not
only provides extremely favorable tax concessions
to holding companies, but it also provides an environment where financial expertise is plentiful,
where communications are easy, and exchange regulations are favorable. In addition, Luxembourg
stands at the center of the Common Market, a point
of considerable interest to many overseas companies.

Fashions change as far as the situation of
holding companies is concerned, but Luxembourg appears to go on forever (although there have been
recent rumblings from France). Liechtenstein was
once popular, but now it is virtually impossible to
set up a new company there; in any case, much adverse publicity has been aired recently regarding the
evil-doings of some Liechtenstein companies, and the
businessman must take care of his financial image.
So, while its tax position is in some respects even
more favorable, Liechtenstein tends to be avoided.

Other holding company environments are provided, for example, by Bermuda, Jamaica, the Bahamas, and (a recent addition), Gibraltar. All these

places have low taxes, but they suffer from one or
another of the disadvantages of inconvenient location or lack of financial expertise. For example,
there is little point in a U.S. holding company for
European operations siting itself in the Bahamas,
where the cost of communications would be greater;
and Gibraltar not only lacks the sophistication of
Luxembourg but is subject to many (and may be subject to even more) exchange-control restrictions as
a member of the sterling area.

TAX CONSIDERATIONS IN LUXEMBOURG

The above examples emphasize that tax is not
the only consideration, but when the picture is
favorable in all other respects, tax does become a
major factor. And in this respect, the businessman
must bear five separate considerations in mind:
first, the problem of taxes in the country where
the income arises; second, the Luxembourg taxes on
overseas income received by the holding company;
third, the Luxembourg taxes on income accumulated
by the holding company; fourth, taxes levied by
Luxembourg on income paid to the overseas parent;
and finally, taxes levied in the parent company's
country.

The first problem is governed by domestic taxation in the country where the income arises, and
then by provisions of any double-tax treaty that
may exist between Luxembourg and the country where
the income arises. Both parts of this problem are
complex, especially with regard to the choice of
site for the holding company (or, indeed, whether
to use a holding company at all). They are discussed in considerable detail in Chapter 5 where,
in particular, it is pointed out that the double-
tax agreements negotiated by Luxembourg exclude
holding companies from the benefits of reduced
rates of withholding tax on dividends, royalties,
and interest--the major flow of income.

In passing, it is worth noting that it may be

possible to arrange the operations of the Luxembourg
holding company so that withholding taxes are irrelevant. For example, ISE Finance, the I. T. & T.
subsidiary, makes loans to other I. T. & T. subsidiaries that are repaid by the delivery of "obligations." These obligations are, in effect, various debts incurred by I. T. & T. customers for the
purchase or rental of equipment, and ISE purchases
such paper at a discount from the subsidiary that
originally entered into contract with the customers.
This set-up is clearly far superior to making direct
loans to the subsidiary, because in this case, withholding tax on interest payments to ISE is irrelevant, with "interest" having been translated into
"discount."

However, the major tax point that the businessman must consider is the second consideration, that
is, what the Luxembourg taxes on overseas income
received by the holding company are. Here the answer is very favorable. There are three taxes, all
of them minute, <u>taxe d'abonnement</u>, <u>droit d'apport</u>,
and <u>droit de timbre</u>. The first is levied on the
average market value over the appropriate year of
all the securities issued by the company: the rate
is 0.16 per cent. The second is levied on the value of the subscribed capital and on the value of
any increase in the capitalization, with a rate of
0.32 per cent, levied only once, at the time of
capitalization. The third is levied on the nominal
value of the shares or other securities issued by
the company; the rate is 0.1 per cent, levied once,
at the time of issue.

Consequently, it is not surprising that Luxembourg is popular. Its three taxes are infinitely
preferable to the "standard" collection of income
taxes, net-worth taxes, and various forms of business and corporation taxes. Furthermore, the tax
bill can be even smaller if the holding company
qualifies as a "holding milliardaire," that is, if
the net assets amount to at least 1 billion Luxembourg francs ($20 million). These companies are
subject only to a single tax on incorporation, and

the annual tax on issued shares (<u>taxe d'abonnement</u>)
is abolished.

The third tax consideration, the problem of
taxes on accumulated income, can be easily disposed
of. Luxembourg holding companies are not subject
to any form of tax on accumulated income. The
fourth consideration, withholding taxes on dividends
and interest paid to the foreign parent (or bondholders in general), is also easily answered. Luxembourg imposes no withholding tax or any other
form of tax on dividends distributed or income paid
to either a foreign parent or a foreign bondholder.

However, the fifth consideration, taxes levied
by the parent company's country on holding-company
dividends, is again extremely complex, since the
treatment of overseas income varies from country to
country and depends on many factors. Chapter 5
provides a detailed discussion of this factor for
the more important countries of issue.

To sum up, it is clear that apart from initial
taxes, the annual tax bill of a standard holding
company is a mere 0.16 per cent on the effective
value of the issued securities. It is interesting
to record the method used by the Luxembourg authorities to estimate this value:

> If the shares issued by the company
> are not quoted, the Revenue authorities
> estimate their effective value from the
> dividend distributed, the par value
> corresponding to a dividend of 10%.
> Thus, if the dividend distributed is
> 20%, the value taken is double the
> nominal value. If the profits are
> large and are transferred in their
> entirety to reserves, a valuation be-
> low par is scarcely likely to be ad-
> mitted, even if the dividend distrib-
> uted is less than 10%. On the other
> hand, the shares of a holding company
> paying a dividend which does not exceed

10% will not be taxed on an above-par
valuation even if the reserves or the
valuation of the securities in the
portfolio should show a large capital
surplus.[5]

Luxembourg, therefore, attracts investors from
the tax point of view, and, as we have seen, the
overseas parent is also attracted by many other
features. Additional points of benefit include a
fairly free legal system meeting all requirements,
the fact that directors and the staff (and audi-
tors) of the holding company may be of foreign nationality and reside abroad, and the fact that
there is no official supervision of the books.

THE OFFERING PROSPECTUS

When we assume that the Luxembourg holding
company has been established, the next marketing
problem is to draw up the offering prospectus. It
should be emphasized that this prospectus will be
drawn up by the firm's bankers and never by the
client.

The actual topics covered are fairly obvious,
and we have already discussed many of them earlier.
First, there is usually a description of the debentures and guarantee (Chapter 2), followed by a description of the offering holding company and comments on the use of proceeds. Then comes the various accounts of both the holding company and the
consolidated group. Figures are usually given over
a period of at least three years for comparison
purposes. In addition to the above accounts and
the necessary auditor's report, a fairly comprehensive history of the parent company is provided.
These contents are, of course, geared to the requirements of the Luxembourg authorities and to the
stock exchanges of various countries on which listings (equivalent to quotations) might be desired;
the latter point is very relevant and is discussed
later. It is impossible to list the regulations of

every stock exchange, especially as disclosure requirements vary widely. In general, Luxembourg
requirements are less stringent than London requirements which, in turn, are less stringent than New
York. Generally, the material that must be published is information on the company's history,
business, management, and current prospects, sup-
ported by an audited report on past profits, assets,
and liabilities. In particular, the prospectus
should include the following: name, domicile, year
of incorporation, activities and plant location of
the issuing company, number of employees, names of
affiliated companies, description of the securities
offered and their various conditions and guarantees,
names and addresses of directors with other direc-
torships, office address, and shareholders' meeting
place, accounts for at least three years, and possible turnover in three years, and often the prospects for the current year.

    The section entitled "underwriting" gives de-
tails of the underwriting agreement and provides a
full list of the underwriters; a "general information" section fills in all details not previously
outlined. For example, the general information
section of the prospectus for the $30 million ICI
loan in March, 1967, deals with the following
headings: quotation of the bonds, consents (exchange control), documents available for inspection,
statutory and other information, agreement with
J. Henry Schroder Wagg & Company Limited, and selling and underwriting.

    The major reason that there is no standard
form of prospectus is that international bond issues, in general, are not subject to domestic law
regarding the nature and content of the information
provided. For example, an issue by a U.S. subsidiary abroad always states: "The debentures have
not been registered under the Securities Act of
1933 of the United States of America and are not
being offered in the U.S.A.," while a United Kingdom prospectus contains a sentence to the effect
that a certificate of exemption has been granted

by the London Stock Exchange under Section 39 of
the 1948 Companies Act. This means that the United
Kingdom company is not bound by the stringent prospectus requirements of the 1948 Companies Act.
This certificate of exemption is required whether
the bonds are to be quoted in London or not. Where
the bonds are not to be quoted, the Stock Exchange
is in fact acting as the agent of the United Kingdom Board of Trade for the purpose of Section 39.
The various domestic regulations covering international bond issues are discussed more fully in
Chapter 4. However, it remains broadly true that
regulation of such issues is not as stringent as
the rules applying to internal issues within the
various countries. The problems of supranational
regulation will be discussed in Chapter 7.

STOCK-EXCHANGE LISTINGS

In fact, one obvious method to allay the fears
of potential investors is to apply for a listing on
one or several stock exchanges. Every stock exchange has fairly stringent listing and disclosure
requirements, and the fact that the company is prepared to submit to them is a guarantee of good
faith as far as investors are concerned. This ex-
plains the enigma of listing (see Chapter 1), which,
on the face of it, is surprising, since such issues
are rarely dealt with on the relevant stock exchanges,* and the more obvious benefits of wider
distribution, advertising, prestige, and so forth,
are not really relevant in many cases. The situation is summed up by Genillard as follows:

> A listing is frequently required for
> an issue to be eligible as an invest-
> ment for certain types of institution-
> al investors, but more importantly, in
> the case of major exchanges, listing

---

*See the discussion below on after-markets.

requirements are a guarantee of proper
and continuing disclosure of financial
information to investors.[6]

There is one other major reason why a listing may
be desired. The fact is that exchange control requirements in the United Kingdom, the Netherlands,
and Italy, make it necessary for bonds to be quoted
on a recognized exchange if they are to be bought
by their own investors respectively (see Chapter 4
for further details). If the bonds are unlisted,
various permissions are required, and the process
of application may be long and drawn out.

In theory, stock exchanges are reluctant to
grant a quotation if all buying and selling is
likely to be conducted off the exchange. In practice, however, this reluctance usually proves temporary because the stock exchange does collect both
an admission fee and an annual maintenance fee for
the quotation. And, in view of the fact that buying and selling via the exchange is likely to be
much more expensive than dealing "net" with brokers
(discussed later), most stock exchanges accept the
fact that the quotation will be for "prestige" and
similar other purposes rather than for "dealing."
Of course, this state of affairs cannot be carried
beyond a certain point, as stock exchanges tend to
be sensitive about their image. For example, the
Luxembourg Stock Exchange still demands that a normal and regular flow of business be conducted in
the stocks they list; but the real state of affairs
is entirely different, as a glance through their
quotation list will show. It is debatable whether
Luxembourg is now a "sleeping" market to a far
greater extent than is desirable. (This problem
will be raised again in the final chapter, where it
is suggested that authorities other than stock exchanges, which are, after all, basically markets,
could provide the necessary prestige and disclosure
requirements.)

UNDERWRITING

We now turn to the underwriting aspects which, as pointed out in Chapter 1, are one of the major distinguishing features of a true international loan. A glance at the underwriting columns in a prospectus gives an indication of the vast spread of these issues and the many and diverse markets that the underwriters hope to tap. For example, the Pepsico Overseas issue, referred to earlier, lists over sixty underwriters in eleven different countries; the Austrian Brenner Autobahn issue lists seven managing underwriters, three in Austria, two in Belgium, one in Italy, one in New York, and thirty-four additional underwriters.

The method of underwriting normally employed is the U.S. pattern, with some variations; the United Kingdom "standby" technique where the underwriters agree for a fee to take up any securities left unsold is rarely employed. What happens is that a group of managers (which may only consist of one firm--for example, the United Kingdom merchant bank, J. Henry Schroder Wagg, was the sole manager of the recent $30 million ICI issue) having formed a team of underwriters, enter into an agreement with the issuing company to purchase all the bonds at an agreed price. This price will stand at a small discount from the ultimate offer price in order to compensate the underwriters for the risks involved, the discount usually being in the range of 2 to 3 per cent. This underwriting group (or "purchase group") then forms a large international selling group to which the bonds are offered at a smaller discount (usually about 1-1/2 per cent), and the selling group in turn can offer the bonds to dealers at a discount of 1/2 per cent.

Consequently, the underwriting columns of a prospectus usually contain such statements as this: "The underwriters have jointly and severally agreed to purchase . . . bonds in the aggregate principal amount of the issue at a purchase price of X per cent of the principal amount thereof plus accrued interest." The selling group is covered by this statement: "The underwriters may offer the debentures to certain dealers at the offering price set forth on the cover page of this offering prospectus less concessions, and such dealers may reallow discounts to other dealers."

A good summary of the entire procedure is provided by the ICI loan mentioned above:

> Under an Agreement dated 15th March 1967, J. Henry Schroder Wagg & Co. Ltd. have agreed to subscribe for the Bonds at a price of 99-1/2% subject to permission to deal in and quotation for the Bonds being granted by the Council of the Stock Exchange, London, not later than 23rd March, 1967. The Company will pay JHSW a commission of 2-3/4% of the nominal amount of the Bonds. The Company will also pay all the expenses of the issue of the Bonds. JHSW are inviting certain banks, brokers, dealers and others [the selling group] to purchase Bonds at the issue price. JHSW will allow a concession of 1-1/2% of the nominal amount of the Bonds to members of the Selling Group, out of which the latter may concede a re-allowance of 1/2% to recognised dealers. Sales of Bonds are being made on condition that they will not, in connection with their distribution, be offered or sold or delivered in the U.S.A. or its territories or possessions or to nationals or residents thereof, or in the United Kingdom or to persons who are residents thereof.

The restriction that the bonds may not be offered in the U.S. is a direct consequence of the fact that the Securities Act of 1933 has not been complied with. The United Kingdom restriction is somewhat more puzzling since, on the face of it, there is no reason why United Kingdom residents should not subscribe with "investment" dollars, paying the premium, then about 20 per cent. However, in this instance, the company specifically forbade United Kingdom subscriptions, although there was no legal reason why they should do so. Presumably, they felt that investor interest would be low in any case owing to the high level of the dollar premium.

A major underwriting problem in any large issue is the time lag between the announcement of the loan and the date on which dealing commences. In this period, underwriters have to find homes for their commitments, and it is clear that considerable upsets could occur if interest rates or other financial events cause a change in conditions. It is obvious that this problem looms particularly large in an international bond issue, and the solution usually employed is, in fact, to keep the terms of the loan fluid until the last possible moment. Investors are not offered bonds at a specific price; they are offered bonds at an unknown price which, they are assured, will reflect market conditions at the time of the issue. Most other details are made public (for example, the conversion premium, if applicable, and the coupon), but the price remains subject to last-minute adjustments.

Clearly, this procedure protects the underwriters; and, provided the investors trust the underwriters, the former should not suffer, despite their act of faith. In one sense, however, the underwriters' job is made more difficult because they sell the issue on the basis of name rather than terms; it might still prove better to announce attractive terms for a smaller company issue, and hope that market conditions do not change. Of course, fixed-price underwriting also has disadvantages. First, there is a tendency to underprice the issue in order to ensure that the underwriters are not left holding an extremely expensive baby, and this is clearly a major risk in the international market. Second, the underwriters are not

only exposed to normal interest rate risks (or
supranormal), they are also exposed to the risks of
currency parities and international political developments. Third, a fixed-price issue might prove
to be a give-away in conditions of booming demand.
In one sense, the fluid-price system employed in
the international market has some similarity to the
U.S. system of testing the market by provisional
selling returns before the underwriting agreement
is actually signed. But it is worth pointing out
that the scales are heavily weighted in favor of
the borrowers rather than the lenders.

It will be noted from the above that the international bond market is mainly a placement market; the public are never invited to subscribe, and
press advertisements are either for information
only or are required for stock-exchange quotation.
This is partly a reflection of the fact that public
interest would in any case be low owing to relative
lack of knowledge in the field and to the undesirable complications of small subscriptions on such
large international issues. In any case, the general public would find it difficult to judge the
merits of any particular issue, especially if they
did not know the price, since yardsticks of comparison are few. So it is as well to leave the
subscription to the bankers who will then suggest
participation to an appropriate client.

As mentioned above, the true international issue can be characterized by its international syndicate of underwriters. Table 11 provides a list
(prepared by White, Weld and Company), of such issues to be compared with Table 12. Following Table
11,a typical list of underwriters (taken from a
recent issue) is given. The presence of United
Kingdom investment houses is due to their entrepôt
function, as outlined in Chapter 1.

The presence of Swiss banks requires further
explanation. Until recently, Swiss banks were notable by their absence from the syndicate; this
was, on the face of it, surprising, since it was

clear that they and their clients accounted for a
large proportion of purchases (discussed later).
In fact, their attitude was governed by the dis-
approval of the Swiss authorities and the fact that
certain tax disadvantages accrued to foreign issues
underwritten in Switzerland. A stamp tax of 1.2
per cent on the nominal value of the issue was required, as was an annual coupon tax of 3 per cent
on interest. Now, however, the Swiss banks have
reached what one commentator calls a "limited modus
vivendi" with the authorities; for example, the
coupon tax has been abolished, and Swiss banks can,
with limitations, subscribe to international issues.
For example, they recently drew down $10 million of
the $30 million ICI issue.[7]

We now turn to a general consideration of current underwriting techniques and secondary markets.
Before doing so, however, it might be well to consider the complex question of demand for these issues. Where does the money come from? As mentioned earlier, underwriters tend to be coy about
their sources of demand, so concrete figures are
impossible to obtain. However, two major points
can be made: first, that institutional interest is
increasing; and second, that a considerable volume
of non-European interest exists.

On the first point, it is fairly evident that
much of the earlier demand had been from wealthy
private individuals (via their banks). This explained the dominant role of Swiss banks, which
certainly purchased as much as 50 per cent of some
issues for their clients' accounts. Tax advantages,
such as no withholding tax, were tailor-made for
such private holdings, and, as a result, the effective net interest rate was higher than could
have been achieved with perfect safety elsewhere.
For example, it was true that a 3-1/2 per cent
United Kingdom War Loan provided a better yield
than an international straight issue; and it was
true that the interest on such a loan was payable
tax-free; but the currency was regarded, rightly,
in view of subsequent events, with considerable

suspicion. Conversely, U.S. tax-free bond issues
provided an excellent safe currency but the yields
were considerably lower. Another important point
is that all international loans are in "bearer"
form.

As the market progressed, institutions began
to take an interest, particularly those with international connections. And this movement has been
aided, not only by the introduction of convertibles
and the increasing volume of available issues, but
also by receding fears that the market was purely
temporary (see Chapter 7). One mutual fund, the
International Income Fund, was established for the
sole purpose of investing in such issues. At the
same time, there is no doubt that the geographical
spread is becoming wider. Much of the initial subscription still comes from Switzerland, but it is
well known that the Swiss bankers are applying on
behalf of not only European clients but Middle
Easterners, Far Easterners, and Central and South
Americans as well "who want the highest rate of
interest consistent with safety paid without deduction of tax."[8]

Ultimately, there is no reason why the supply
of funds coming into the international bond market
should not be equal in quantity, quality, and
spread to any major national market. Clearly, this
market had a prime initial attraction to "refugee"
money; but this, while carrying the taint of immo-
rality, is not to be condemned, since supranational
safety is often more financially desirable than
national unsafety and restrictive practices; and
the quality of these issues is in many cases extremely high. The major problem of the extent to
which European capital markets have been stimulated
by international bonds (or vice versa) is examined
later.

If the market is to equal a major national
market in efficiency, safety, and so forth, the
secondary markets are of prime importance; and here
there is no doubt that international bond markets

do not accord to the highest ideals. To some measure, this is a reflection of the underwriting
techniques used, which should place the stock in
firm hands, thus making the stimulation of after-
market dealing* extremely difficult. In practice,
underwriters often place the stock in unsettled
temporary hands. This is even worse, since what
happens is that these "buyers" who are in for a
quick profit dispose of the stock at the first possible opportunity, thus clogging the market. Examples abound of perfectly reasonable bond issues
that have been badly placed and tend to drift lower
because of a surfeit of "stag" selling. To those
in the trade, the culprits are well known and tend
to gather in certain European centers.

Consequently, the international bond market is
to some extent on the horns of a dilemma; if the
issues are well placed, little turnover occurs; if
they are not, the market is depressed. And this
factor, together with rising interest rates, was
sufficient to depress prices by about 7 per cent in
1966. It might well be suggested that the international bond market is really no different from the
United Kingdom gilt market, where turnover is huge.
What is wrong? The fact is that the market is not
yet sufficiently large, and, in any case, the issues are too diverse to provide any concrete
"switching" criteria. For example, it is compara-
tively easy to decide when United Kingdom Treasury
at 5-1/2 per cent 2008/2012 is expensive in relation to funding 3-1/2 per cent 1999/2004; but it
is much harder to know when to switch into a Portugese guaranteed issue from a New Zealand Government
Loan, for example. At what precise price differential is the former cheap? Consequently, holders
tend to stay put.

It is inevitable that switching criteria are
much more applicable to a national market. The tax

---

*Trading of bonds after the original purchase.

system is uniform, and furthermore, the varying effects of the tax system on different types of institutions provide a major stimulus to switching.
In addition, the underlying security of government
stocks is similar, and it is thus much simpler to
decide when "yield" differentials, however defined,
get out of line. Last, but not least, government
monetary policy, such as a "tap" of gilt-edged issues, often provides a basis for switching, while
the domestic interest rate structure is clearly
defined.

This tap factor is notably absent in international markets, and the security of the various
issues differs widely. To date, the diverse needs
of the various institutions are not yet channeled
to the international bond market in sufficient
quantity to establish firm price differentials for
all the issues. In any case, the different degrees
of security offered have not yet been precisely
evaluated, while an international interest structure, although in an embryonic stage (see Chapter
6), is not sufficiently well defined.

This state of affairs will alter gradually as
the market develops, and several other factors will
also help. First, there will be a constantly increasing stream of sinking fund and interest payments on outstanding loans. This money will tend
to return to the market. Second, brokers, whose
bread and butter lies in commission, are naturally
interested in stimulating turnover and produce cir-
culars from time to time outlining anomalies. For
example, Strauss, Turnbull, leading London brokers,
have produced at least two interesting notices, one
of which attempts to produce a method of assessing
different convertible issues.[9] Finally, there is
no doubt that the after-market has been bedeviled
by a succession of temporary upsets recently, such
as the rise in interest rates, market congestion,
and so forth.

At some stage, no doubt, the switching criteria
will become clearly defined, and an active market

will develop. However, despite the improvement
since the beginning of 1967, it is sometimes difficult to deal in these bonds. Dealings are usually
accomplished direct, via brokers, and net prices
are quoted. But while there may be no problem in
selling $50,000 of the recent ICI issue, for exam-
ple, considerable time, even a matter of months,
perhaps, could elapse before a buyer is found for
the same quantity of Takeda Chemical, the Japanese
issue. Of course, the major houses deal as prin-
cipals, but, in practice, they will not open any
position that they feel they cannot close again
fairly quickly.

THE IMPORTANCE OF AFTER-MARKETS

Therefore, although the full development of
after-markets is, in part, a long-term process and
cannot be hurried, one or two things could be accomplished immediately. First, wider publication
of the relevant quotations is desirable, and this
not only implies stock-exchange listings but also a
listing in relevant leading financial newspapers.
Both The New York Times and the London Financial
Times are deficient in this respect. Second, some
effort could be made to overhaul placing procedures; a penalty clause that forces the itinerant
buyer to pay for his sins should be standard, and
managing underwriters should employ after-market
stabilization techniques. Genillard suggests that
the relative absence of the latter is due, in part,
to the conflict of interest when the investment
banker and the commercial banker are one and the
same, but the effort should still be made. Third,
a much more positive attempt should be made to rate
international issues so that switching becomes possible; at present, most investment houses find it
much more lucrative to manage issues rather than to
make markets in them, but making market is part of
the job of management.

Finally, a wide range of paying agents is essential, so that holders can obtain their interest

payments with a minimum of trouble. Indeed, most bonds are fairly adequate in this respect; for example, the Beeching issue states:

> The debenture and coupons may be presented for payment in dollars (a) at the corporate trust office of the First National City Bank in New York or (b) subject to any applicable laws in the country concerned, at the offices of First National City Bank in London, Brussels, Amsterdam, Paris, Frankfurt, or Milan or at the office of Banque Europeene du Luxembourg in Luxembourg. Payment at the offices referred to in (b) above will be made by a dollar cheque drawn on a bank in New York City or by a transfer to a Dollar account maintained by the payee with a bank in New York City.

One matter that has not been considered above is the effect of national exchange control and currency restrictions on demand. It would appear obvious that the more people are permitted to buy these loans free of restrictions, the more the market will develop. On the other hand, reversing the coin, without the interest-equalization tax, the market would never have developed at all. Certainly, a general relaxation of European restrictions would ease matters; but this implies free convertibility of the domestic currency, and other economic consequences. The entire subject is discussed in Chapter 5.

NOTES TO CHAPTER 3

1. For example, see J. S. G. Wilson, "Some Aspects of the Development of Capital Markets," Quarterly Review (Banco Nazionale de Lavoro) (December, 1966), p. 263.

2.   Banque Internationale a Luxembourg, Holding Companies in the Grand Duchy of Luxembourg (1959), p. 13.

3.   "Two Snags on the Dollar Bond Floor," Business International (March 18, 1966).

4.   Banque Internationale a Luxembourg, op. cit., p. 13.

5.   Ibid., p. 26.

6.   "The European Capital Market," Federal Trust Report, Special Series No. 2 (London, 1967), p. 39.

7.   Federal Reserve Bank of New York, "Recent Developments in the International Capital Market" (October, 1966), p. 225.

8.   John Chown and Robert Valentine, "Tapping Europe's Millions," Management Today (July-August, 1966).

9.   Research Department of Strauss, Turnbull, "A Technical Study of Convertible Euro-bonds" (London, March, 1967).

4

RESTRICTIONS ON THE MOVEMENT OF INTERNATIONAL CAPITAL AND EFFECTS ON THE MARKET

The Euro-bond market owes its origin to restrictions on international capital movements, although the market, now created, will almost certainly continue to flourish even if the restrictions are removed. In this chapter, we will analyze in detail the relevant restrictions on the movement of capital between countries.

BACKGROUND INFORMATION

Many countries impose rigid exchange control regulations that virtually preclude their citizens from investing legally in foreign securities or holding assets abroad. A substantial part of the funds invested in the international market may belong to citizens of such countries who, with reason, distrust their own governments and currencies and have succeeded in transferring funds or retaining earnings abroad. A perverse but inevitable consequence of such restrictions is an increased volume of migratory funds that seek to avoid future exchange restrictions and taxes. Traditional havens for such funds have been Switzerland, Panama, Hong Kong, and the Bahamas but sophisticated owners may sometimes find that London and New York offer better facilities and just as much freedom for nonresidents.

Certain advanced countries, notably the United States and the United Kingdom, impose complex, sophisticated, and flexible restrictions on capital movements, seeking to protect their balance of payments with minimum disturbance to the extensive and profitable international business carried on by their citizens and resident corporations. Such other countries as Germany and Switzerland do not directly restrict capital movements but do take measures to protect the autonomy of their internal monetary policy.

Rigid restrictions of the first type need little comment other than to say that they exist.[1] The more complex regulations of countries that are international business centers vitally affect the structure and development of the international bond market and will be analyzed in considerable detail below.

In certain countries such as Canada and France, steps are taken to discourage what they regard as excessive foreign investment in their countries.[2] They are not so much concerned with their balance of payments as with maintaining their national character and preventing excessive foreign managerial and financial control. There are pressures for similar policies in other countries. This factor does not directly influence the international bond market and is therefore not discussed in detail here. The existence of the market is giving a new stimulus to the movement of capital and management between countries, and a possible reaction could be an increase in economic nationalism, a force very much the concern of international businessmen and investors.

In theory, the U.S. dollar is fully convertible, and the U.S. does not impose any exchange control restrictions on its citizens. Nevertheless, the U.S. has succeeded in imposing obstacles to international capital movements more illiberal than any major industrial country except the United Kingdom. U.S. restrictions take two forms. The interest-equalization tax applies to portfolio investments, while the voluntary guidelines program restricts bank loans and direct investment.

THE INTEREST-EQUALIZATION TAX

The interest-equalization tax (IET) was introduced on July 19, 1963,[3] and U.S. citizens, resident aliens, or resident corporations purchasing
securities after that date are liable to an excise
tax. In the case of redeemable bonds, the tax is
on a sliding scale at a rate varying with the period from purchase or subscription to maturity.
The scale was calculated effectively to reduce the
yield on a security purchased and held to redemption by about 1 per cent. For bonds that are ir-
redeemable or that have a life exceeding 28-1/2
years and for stocks the rate of tax was 15 per
cent. The new act[4] alters the regulations and increases the rates. For the period from January 25,
1967, to August 29, 1967, the rate was increased to
22.5 per cent on stocks and by a corresponding
amount on dated bonds to give an interest differential of approximately 1.5 per cent. The act provided that after August 29, 1967, the President
could by executive order vary the rate between 0
and a maximum of 22.5 per cent. It was in fact
reduced on that date to 18.75 per cent for stocks
and correspondingly for bonds.

The IET has fulfilled the purpose implicit in
its title in relation to bonds. Prior to its introduction, the generally lower rate of bond interest in the U.S. and the enormous funds available
in its capital market were very attractive to the
foreign issuer who had access to the New York market. The IET neutralized that advantage, and a
coupon high enough to attract the European investor
was not quite enough to compensate U.S. purchasers
for the tax. For a time in 1966, interest rates in
Europe reached a level at which it once more became attractive to borrow in the U.S. The peak had
passed by the following year, and the reduction of
the IET rate from 22.5 per cent to 18.75 per cent
is unlikely to make any difference.

It is generally agreed that the introduction
of IET gave the first impetus to the development of

the Euro-bond market.   Bankers in London and elsewhere in Europe seized the opportunity to attract
business away from New York. As explained earlier,
the first real Euro-bond issue was made three weeks
<u>before</u> the introduction of the tax.

There are many exceptions to the IET. Logically enough, stocks purchased from other U.S. owners are exempt.[5] There are exemptions for public
and private issues from less developed countries.[6]
Canadian securities have been exempted and some
concessions are given to Japan.[7] However, since
September 12, 1966, the tax <u>has</u> applied to the acquisition of the securities of a Canadian corporation, partnership, or trust formed (or availed of)
to acquire securities from a Canadian or other foreign issuer.[8] This provision sought to close an
obvious loophole. Direct investments abroad,
whether in the form of branches or subsidiaries,
are not subject to IET.[9]

If the IET has lived up to its name in the
case of bonds, it has had a very unfortunate history in its effect on dealings in stocks. It is,
in effect, a once-and-for-all penalty on the purchase of stocks from foreign corporations that
make the odds against successful investment intol-
erably high. Although the investor might in principle recover part of the tax by selling the security to another American investor at a premium, in
practice the premium varies with the individual
stock, and there are no facilities for switching
within a general pool comparable to the United
Kingdom premium dollar and the South African
blocked-Rand markets (see page 96).   Such restrictions on the proper management of portfolio investments would be intolerable except for the sheer
size of the U.S. internal market and the lack of a
real tradition of international portfolio investment. The tax has been a major blow to the role
of the U.S. in the development of a free and sophisticated international capital market.

If the IET has been a body blow to honest

investors, it has proved a bonanza for dishonest
operators. They bought blocks of British and European stocks in which there was an active U.S. market. They then either forged certificates of American ownership or arranged for them to be signed
fraudulently by a man of straw, often a U.S. citi-
zen living permanently in Canada, Mexico, or the
Caribbean. The stock was then unloaded through the
market at a premium to innocent investors. Most
people in the securities business in Europe have
seen at least indirect evidence of this huge industry, and estimates of the profits have ranged from
$100 million to $1 billion.   It seems incredible
that the U.S. Internal Revenue Service has accepted
certificates of this kind without any form of in-
vestigation into the prior history of the stock or
the identity of the person signing the certificate.
It was apparently possible to pick up forms at any
IRS office; anyone prepared to perjure himself
could manufacture valuable certificates very easily
indeed. But on July 31, 1967, a new validation
procedure (intended to be retroactive) was introduced in an attempt to block this astonishing loophole.[10]

THE VOLUNTARY GUIDELINES PROGRAM

        Direct investment abroad by U.S. corporations
is exempt from the IET, and it was felt that these
were becoming a major drain on the U.S. balance of
payments. On February 10, 1965, therefore, the
President presented a program to Congress to improve the U.S. balance of payments.[11] This program
included amendments to the IET, reduced the duty-
free allowance of returning tourists, sought to encourage a "see the U.S.A. first" approach to tour-
ism, and foreshadowed what became The Foreign Investors Tax Act, designed to remove obstacles to
foreign investment in the U.S. The message also
introduced the voluntary guidelines program under
which business concerns, banks, and other financial
institutions were encouraged to cooperate in reducing the balance-of-payments deficit.

As a first step in this program, the Secretary of Commerce wrote to the chief executives of some 600 corporations engaged in international business, seeking their cooperation. They were asked to prepare a balance-of-payments ledger in accordance with a summary worksheet enclosed with the letter, on exports, royalties, capital movements, and foreign profits. In accordance with the recommendation of the Advisory Committee of "outstanding leaders from the business community" the program was to be kept on as an informal and personal a basis as possible. It specifically provided that restraint on foreign investment was to apply only to investment in the developed countries, then defined as Australia, Austria, Belgium, Canada, Denmark, France, Germany, Hong Kong, Italy, Japan, Liechtenstein, Luxembourg, Monaco, Netherlands, New Zealand, Norway, South Africa, San Marino, Spain, Sweden, Switzerland, and the United Kingdom. (The following year Abu Dhabi, Bahrain, Indonesia, Iran, Iraq, Libya, Qatar, Kuwait, and Saudi Arabia were added.) It was recognized that Canada represented a special problem, as she is largely dependent on U.S. industrial investment. Firms did not have to cut-back direct investment in Canada but were asked to take particular care to ensure that funds put at the disposal of subsidiaries in Canada were used to meet operating needs in Canada.

On December 6, 1965, the 1966 program was announced. An additional 400 companies were invited to join the voluntary program. Information provided by businesses enabled more specific guidelines to be laid down. The target recommended was that direct investment in the combined two-year period of 1965-66 should be limited to 90 per cent of the amount during the three-year period of 1962-64. Direct investment was defined to include the net outflow of funds from the U.S. plus undistributed profits of subsidiaries abroad. In effect, the annual average for the two years was permitted to be 35 per cent above the annual average during the base period. For the first time, restraint was requested on direct investment in Canada. The 1967 goal was somewhat tighter, and businesses were requested to limit investment to an annual average rate of 20 per cent (instead of 35 per cent) above the average of the 1962-64 base period.

It should be noted that there are no restrictions on expansion by borrowing abroad, and indeed announcements in 1968 particularly stressed that the intention was not to cut back on the activities of U.S. companies but to encourage them to raise finances locally. It need hardly be stressed that these restrictions and this attitude have been major factors in encouraging the use of the Euro-bond market by U.S. business. Corporations have been particularly asked to absorb the higher interest cost of such borrowing as part of their contribution to the balance-of-payments program.

The cooperation of banks was also sought. In the original 1965 program, banks were asked to restrain credits to foreigners who were not clearly and directly financing exports of U.S. goods and services and to limit outstanding credits to foreigners (including export credits) during 1965 to a level not more than 5 per cent above the amount outstanding on December 31, 1964. Priority was to be given first to export credits and then to credits to assist underdeveloped countries. Banks were asked to give special consideration to Canada and Japan, as both are highly dependent on U.S. finance, and to recognize that the United Kingdom was going through a difficult period in its own balance of payments. These guidelines were communicated to the banks through the Federal Reserve System in the form of documents that seem clear, helpful, and comprehensive. Similar letters were sent to non-banking financial institutions to ensure that they too cooperated in the program and that business turned away by the banks was not refinanced elsewhere.

The 1966 program raised the guideline to 109 per cent of the December 31, 1964, level, but banks were requested to utilize the permitted expansion

at a rate of not more than 1 per cent per calendar
quarter. For 1967, the 109 per cent ceiling was
retained, but there was an overriding restriction
limiting a bank's lending to its actual funds outstanding on September 30, 1966, plus a quarterly
percentage of the unused potential at that date.
The effect of this was to leave U.S. banks with
only $120 million to lend to developed countries
above the September, 1966, level. Nonbanking financial institutions were permitted to increase
their foreign lending in December, 1967, by 5 per
cent over the base date of September 30, 1966.

The combined effect of IET and the bank and
business guidelines program has been substantially
to check the outflow of capital from the U.S., to
exclude European borrowers from the New York market, and to force U.S. companies expanding in
Europe and elsewhere to seek non-U.S. finance.
Europe has taken over much of New York's role as
a financial entrepôt, and impetus has been given
to a real international capital market.

EXCHANGE CONTROL ACTS IN THE UNITED KINGDOM

The Exchange Control Act of 1947 virtually
prohibits all transactions between residents of
the United Kingdom sterling area and nonresidents,
without Bank of England consent.[12] Most current
transactions and many categories of capital transactions are the subject of general consents, but
these can be varied by administrative order without
prior notice, without the need for legislation, and
without any formal opportunity for Parliament to
object. Those matters requiring specific consent
are in theory considered by the Bank of England on
their merits, but inevitably the officials concerned draw up rules of behavior for themselves,
that with the passing of time have become the
equivalent of unpublished regulations. It is
therefore impossible to state what the exact rules
are now or have been in the past, although current

Bank of England practice is usually fairly well
understood within the banking community. Pressure
for the publication of more precise regulations is
strongly resisted by the Bank and sometimes by the
managers of foreign exchange departments of commercial banks, who value their special relationship
and the mystique created by the lack of publicity.

This situation must be objectionable to those
who believe in the rule of law and who expect any
restrictions on individual freedom to be openly
discussed and publicly justified. In practice, the
Bank of England usually fulfills its role liberally
and intelligently. Fuller publication of exact
rules might even limit the Bank's freedom of action
and incite demands for even more frustrating restrictions from various politicians who are guided
by emotion rather than a rational analysis of facts.

Current transactions between United Kingdom
residents and nonresidents are settled at the official exchange rate, which fluctuates in the market between $2.78 and $2.82 per £1 sterling until
November 19, 1967, when the pound was devalued to a
rate of $2.40. (Subsequent developments are dis-
cussed in Chapter 7.) There are active spot and
forward exchange markets in London between the
pound sterling and most major currencies, and the
mechanics of dealing in practice is not impeded by
the existence of exchange control.

Until recently there were two unofficial but
legal markets for the settlement of capital transactions. These were frequently confused even by
bankers and traders within the United Kingdom. For
the inward movement of capital, there was the
blocked, switch, or security sterling market. For
years, the discount had been minute and its practical effects negligible. It was an annoying technicality that had to be explained to foreigners,
and in April, 1967, this variety of sterling was
sensibly merged with external sterling, simplifying
the procedure (and shortening necessary discussion
here).

For the outward movement of capital, there is
still the premium or investment dollar market. The
theory of this market is that there exists a pool
of foreign investments held by sterling area residents. Residents are free to switch from one investment to another, or to sell the premium dollars
resulting from a sale to other residents at a free
market price. The dollars can only be used for
portfolio investment and cannot (for instance) be
spent on vacations abroad. The securities (or currency awaiting reinvestment) must remain in the
custody or control of a bank, broker, or other authorized depository in the United Kingdom. The
premium recently rose to more than 30 per cent over
the official rate. The same premium over the appropriate official rate applies to the purchase of
investments denominated in French, German, Japanese,
or other foreign currencies. Unlike the U.S.
interest-equalization tax discussed above, part
(previously all) of the premium is recoverable on
a sale, but as dividends and interest are paid at
the official rate, one effect of the premium is
substantially to reduce the yield on nonsterling
securities. Prior to April, 1965, the premium
simply reflected an exchange rate in a secondary
market, and the seller of securities could sell the
resulting foreign currency at the premium rate.
Since April, 1965, sellers have had to surrender a
quarter of the proceeds at the official rate, but
they are still able to obtain the premium on the
balance of the remaining three quarters.[13] Alternatively, this balance can be retained temporarily
for later investment, but a quarter of the balance
not sold or reinvested must be surrendered at the
end of each six-month period. Such funds awaiting
reinvestment can be deposited at interest or used
to buy certain types of money-market paper (including Euro-dollar certificates of deposit issued by
the London offices of U.S. and other banks), without the sale or redemption at maturity of the paper
resulting in an obligation to surrender.

The United Kingdom buyer of an international
bond at $100 with a 6 per cent coupon would (at a

25 per cent premium) have to pay the equivalent of
$125 and would therefore find his yield reduced to
4.8 per cent. If both the price of the security
and the premium remained unchanged, he would receive only 118-3/4 on the sale of the bond, a loss
of 6-1/4 points. He would lose even more if the
premium were to fall, and it may immediately be
seen that the existence of a premium at this level
virtually rules out purchases by United Kingdom and
other sterling area residents of international
bonds, with the possible exception of a few convertibles.

In spite of the premium, U.S., Canadian, and
other foreign equities are actively bought and sold
by British investors who (except for the premium)
have ready and convenient access to Wall Street.
As such investments are unattractive on yield
grounds, the appeal is for capital gain. It is
obvious that British investors would prefer a highly leveraged situation, and they therefore find the
separately dealtin share-purchase warrants attached
to a bond issue most appealing. The Societa
Generale Immobiliare (SGI) warrants were an example: Oddly, no U.S. issuer took advantage of this
intriguing situation.

British insurance companies are granted substantial practical freedom in the management of
foreign-currency investments held against written
foreign business. They are believed to be substantial investors in the Euro-dollar and Euro-bond
markets.

No specific consent is required for the purchase of listed securities, provided that currency
is purchased in the premium market and the stock
is held by an authorized depository such as a bank,
stockbroker, or solicitor in the United Kingdom.
Investment in unquoted securities and direct investments in foreign subsidiaries and branch operations require the specific consent of the Bank of
England acting as agent for the Treasury. Prior
to May, 1962, consent for direct investment

authorized the investing company to buy currency at
the official rate, but by that date, regulations
had been tightened to the point at which permission
was only being granted to investments with a pay-
back period in foreign exchange terms (including
any benefit to exports) of two to three years.
This stringent requirement ruled out most normal
industrial investments, and it was therefore provided that permission might be granted for generally sound projects that did not meet these stringent
requirements, provided that foreign exchange was
purchased through the premium dollar market. The
premium at that time was only about 3 per cent, but
purchases by industrial investors soon forced it
upward. During 1965, regulations were tightened
still further, and after July of that year, no
direct investment at all was permitted at the official rate. All new investments therefore had to
be financed either by buying dollars in the premium
market or by borrowing abroad. Since May, 1966, it
has been possible to obtain permission to make direct investments even through the premium market
only if it can be shown that <u>short-term</u> benefits
will accrue. This has left foreign borrowing as
the main source of funds for expansion. Bank of
England consent is required for such borrowing:
This is because a parent-company guarantee is a
contingent liability on the reserves, and an
increase in the gearing or leverage of foreign-
investment holdings may postpone the time when a
return can be expected to the reserves. Permission
for borrowing abroad has, on the whole, been fairly
generously granted.

The Bank of England has always had power under
Section 30 of the Exchange Control Act of 1947 to
direct United Kingdom resident individuals or companies controlling non-United Kingdom companies to
use their control to insure that the non-United
Kingdom company pays a dividend, realizes assets,
or repatriates funds. This had been regarded as a
reserve favor, but by 1966 or 1967, the Bank had
been requesting United Kingdom companies operating
abroad to remit a substantial part of their profits

as dividends. For an expanding group, this can
result in a serious loss on exchange. Before devaluation, $1 million remitted at $2.80 produced
£357,142. If the company then wished to reinvest
$1 million abroad, it would have to pay £446,427,
at $2.80, plus a 25 per cent premium, a loss of
£89,285.* The Bank actually suggests that a
directed company might prefer to bypass the dividend procedure by buying $1 million on the premium
dollar market and surrendering this sum at the official rate. This achieves the desired foreign
exchange position directly without the possibly
adverse tax consequences, at home and overseas, of
actually paying a dividend. If it were not for
this, there could be a considerable advantage to a
United Kingdom company in setting up a nonsterling
holding company to permit earnings in one foreign
subsidiary, to be extracted for reinvestment in
another, without a heavy loss on exchange. This
loss is a major factor in corporate planning by
United Kingdom based groups and in spite of it, a
holding company might still give some improvement
in flexibility. It is believed to have been one
of the reasons why Beecham chose to make an international issue through a Luxembourg subsidiary,
although every other United Kingdom borrower to
date had made a direct issue.

As explained above, United Kingdom companies
require exchange control consent even for foreign
investment that is to be financed by overseas borrowing, although this is granted fairly freely.
It is cheaper to borrow abroad in dollars or Swiss
francs than to borrow 30 per cent more in the
United Kingdom (at a higher interest rate too, as
it happens), to buy the same sum in the premium
dollar market. It is not necessary to raise the
loan through a separate subsidiary. The Bank can
agree that a company raises a direct loan in a

----

*These figures, but not the principle, are af-
fected by the devaluation.

foreign currency for an overseas purpose. The mere
fact that it is denominated in a foreign currency
effectively prevents the loan from being financed
indirectly by United Kingdom investors. In spite
of these advantages, relatively few United Kingdom
companies had taken advantage of the market by
1968. One factor has perhaps been the fear of devaluation, which would correspondingly increase
the cost of servicing the loans. The biggest borrower to date had been British Petroleum, which
raised separate loans in Deutsche marks, Swiss
francs, and U.S. dollars.

A special problem arises on the issue by a
foreign subsidiary of a United Kingdom corporation
of a bond convertible into the stock of the parent
company. In foreign-exchange terms, conversion is
equivalent to the repayment of the loan by the
parent company (an outflow of money across the exchanges that would normally require the purchase
of premium dollars), and the simultaneous subscription by nonresidents for shares in the United Kingdom company (that would come over the exchanges at
the official rate). If a company were to issue £1 million of new shares (regardless of whether they were
subscribed by residents or nonresidents) and invest
this money in Europe, the dollar premium would be
payable. In strict logic, therefore, when a convertible loan was converted, the Bank of England
should require that the company purchase dollars
equivalent to the amount of the conversion in the
premium market and surrender these at the official
rate. In the case of the only such issue to 1968
(Beecham International, S.A.) the Bank of England
waived their right in this respect. If the Bank
were less generous in future, the solution might
be to issue bonds with warrants attached. The
stripped bonds would have an appeal to the fixed-
interest market, while the warrants themselves
would enable U.S. investors to take an equity view
on the company with a minimum impact of interest-
equalization tax. The exercise of the warrant
would bring in money at the official rate, and no
United Kingdom problem would arise. In practice,

U.S. residents would never exercise and incur IET. They would take their profit by selling to arbitrageurs outside the U.S. who would exercise and sell stock on the United Kingdom market.

Permission under the Exchange Control Act is required for a sterling area resident to make loans to a nonresident or to a company that, although itself resident, is controlled by nonresidents. Until 1965, ordinary bank borrowing by branches and subsidiaries of foreign companies operating in the United Kingdom were not subject to special restrictions and were not treated separately from domestic borrowings in statistical returns. In 1965, the banks were instructed to make a return of such lending and the regulations are now being used to ensure that they do not become excessive. Ordinary commercial lending still appears to be allowed, but if a U.S. company (itself restricted by guidelines) tried to persuade a United Kingdom bank to make a loan to its subsidiary of a size that could only be justified by the parent guarantee, the Bank of England would step in. This is a clear example of "beggar-my-neighbor" policies in international finance. The Bank of England prefers controlled companies to borrow from abroad in proportion to their foreign shareholding, and there has even been talk of directing listed companies to obtain finance abroad in proportion to their nonresident shareholding.

In addition to the formal exchange control requirements detailed above, the United Kingdom has also followed the U.S. example in adopting a voluntary program of restraint. Exchange control does not directly apply to investments in the rest of the sterling area, but in May, 1966, United Kingdom companies were asked voluntarily to impose on their overseas investment projects in the developed countries of the sterling area (Australia, New Zealand, South Africa, and Ireland) the same limitations legally enforced by exchange control. They were asked to postpone any investments that did not meet the criteria, or alternatively to seek finance for such projects by borrowing outside the United Kingdom. This voluntary program was fairly effective in achieving its ends.

Institutional investors, including investment trusts and unit trusts (mutual funds), were also asked to ensure that there was no net increase in their holdings of securities for the four countries above. They were later asked similarly to limit their total nonsterling holdings.

Closed and investment trusts are much commoner in the United Kingdom than in the U.S., although the real expansion in recent years has been in unit trusts or mutual funds.[14] The old, established, closed-end trusts have been successful investors in U.S. and Canadian securities and have often constituted 30 per cent of their portfolios. The voluntary guidelines and the 25 per cent surrender rule have been a major blow. Both can be bypassed by borrowing dollars (with the consent of the Bank of England). The trusts arrange for a bank loan (usually for five years) against the security of part of their North American portfolios. This provides new money for overseas investment outside the guidelines. The premium is avoided on money borrowed abroad and service can be arranged out of income. The securities so pledged can be switched freely without surrender, and naturally enough, those securities that may need to be switched are transferred to provide the security. As recently as 1968, no such trust had attempted to make a public bond issue, as short-term borrowing meets their needs better, but such an issue, perhaps of five-year bonds, is possible in the future.

Trusts borrowing in this way could, if they wished, operate in the Euro-bond market. As the object is capital gain rather than income (because of the tax position) investments are likely to be limited to convertibles, temporary investments during a bear market for equities, and short-term dealings in anomalies.

THE REMAINDER OF THE STERLING AREA

Apart from the voluntary guidelines discussed above, there are no exchange-control restrictions on transactions by United Kingdom residents in the rest of the sterling area. Other members of the area undertake to impose similar restrictions, and in principle it should be impossible legally to remove funds outside the area via other member countries. In the past, there have been sophisticated leaks through Kuwait and Hong Kong, and illegal transactions are often (for reasons of practical convenience) conducted in small outlying colonies with an essentially dollar economy.

Some member countries, such as the Republic of Ireland and the British Caribbean islands, follow the United Kingdom example and impose no restrictions on transactions with the rest of the sterling area. Some, for example, the Bahamas, have never imposed the 25 per cent premium surrender rule. In this case, action was quickly taken to ensure that dealings in "pre-zero" dollars without surrender were confined to "genuine Bahamians," including Bahamas personal trusts and holding companies, provided these were not set up or acquired by United Kingdom or Irish residents after April 6, 1965.

Other member countries such as India, Pakistan, and Ghana impose the type of rigid restrictions on their own residents that fall outside the scope of our discussion here.

Australia, New Zealand, and South Africa are the most notable examples of major sterling-area countries that impose detailed but flexible restrictions on dealings with residents of other member countries. Australia has long limited the right of its residents to invest abroad. United Kingdom and U.S. restrictions referred to above have cut off a source of capital and forced foreign-controlled companies to borrow locally: Regulations now seriously limit the borrowing powers of foreign-controlled companies in Australia, another example of "beggar-my-neighbor."

The Republic of South Africa has been a substantial net importer of capital but has an active
and sophisticated capital market of its own.
Exchange-control restrictions against the rest of
the sterling area were first imposed in 1961, mainly to forestall a flight of capital. Many securities of South African companies are actively dealt
in on both the London and Johannesburg stock exchanges. Under the restrictions, when a non-South
African sells securities on the Johannesburg market,
proceeds are blocked and in principle can be used
only for the purchase of further quoted securities
in South Africa. Stocks traded in both centers immediately went to a discount in London as against
Johannesburg, and for a few months there were extremely profitable opportunities for the quick-
witted to take advantage of the different discounts
ruling on different stocks. The market soon settled down, and there is now an active market in
blocked-Rand balances. A United Kingdom resident
wishing to buy a South African security can either
buy on the London market or purchase on the Johannesburg market with blocked Rands purchased at a
discount. Arbitrage keeps the effective prices in
line. From time to time, the South African Government has permitted some controlled release of
blocked Rands by issues of 3- to 5-year bonds sub-
scribable in blocked Rands but repayable in sterling freely transferable to the rest of the sterling area. These have proved popular investments,
not for those who accidentally had blocked balances,
but by United Kingdom residents in high-tax brack-
ets who bought blocked Rands especially to invest
for the capital redemption element.

De Beers and ESCOM are two South African companies that have made direct U.S. dollar issues on
the Euro-bond market. Another South African company, Highveldt Steel, made a DM issue with warrants attached. The Queensland Alumina issue
(discussed on page 118) was made to finance Australian expansion, and the governments of Australia,
New Zealand, Ireland, and South Africa have all
made issues on the market.

THE EUROPEAN ECONOMIC COMMUNITY

It is an obvious and necessary aim of any common market to eliminate internal restrictions on capital movements. Article 67 of the Treaty of Rome states:

> During the transitional period and to the extent necessary to ensure the proper functioning of the Common Market, Member States shall progressively abolish between themselves restrictions on the movement of capital belonging to persons resident in Member States and any discrimination based on the nationality or on the place of residence of the parties or on the place where such capital is invested.
>
> Current payments connected with movements of capital between Member States shall be free from all restrictions not later than the end of the first stage.[15]

Although the EEC is in general more liberal in its attitude to capital movements than either the U.S. or the United Kingdom, three countries (France, Italy, and the Netherlands), still impose some restrictions on capital movements even within the EEC; Germany, without actual exchange controls, succeeds in maintaining an autonomous monetary policy with a higher interest-rate structure. Two directives[16] divide capital movements into four categories. Categories A and B are now unconditionally liberalized, and restrictions can only be imposed in accordance with the stringent emergency requirements of Articles 73 and 104 to 109. Category C is conditionally liberalized, which means that member states may maintain restrictions already imposed but may not introduce or tighten up such restrictions except in accordance with the safeguards mentioned above. Category D lists capital movements where restrictions are still allowed.

A third directive[17] was presented by the Commission to the Council. It was still under discussion in 1968, but it will soon be possible to adopt it by qualified majority. The principal effect of the third directive will be to eliminate obstacles to access of capital markets. It is hoped that the securities of one member country will be freely admitted to listing on the stock exchange of another, but at the least, members may have to commit themselves in permitting foreign issues to the extent of 1-1/2 per cent of their gross-capital formation.

The principal categories of investment that have already been unconditionally liberalized are the acquisition of quoted securities by nonresidents and the acquisition by residents of nonresident-quoted securities, except where the obligation is listed on a foreign market but in national currency. Mutual funds are still excluded from Categories A and B. Direct investment of a nonfinancial nature and the purchase of real estate are also permitted, as are personal transfers of capital in connection with emigration or as gifts, dowries, inheritances, or the home remittances of people working abroad. Items conditionally liberalized in Category C include the issue and placement of securities on the markets of another member country and freedom of investment for mutual funds and other financial intermediaries. France, Italy, and the Netherlands are the only countries still imposing such restrictions, and if the third directive is adopted in its present draft form, these will have to go. Category C also includes certain forms of commercial credit and the acquisition for investment purposes of unquoted securities; the third directive does not propose modification of this position.

Category D, where members are free to retain and impose restrictions, mainly affect short-term capital movements such as the purchase of money-market paper, the opening of current bank accounts in other member countries, and the granting of personal loans to nonresidents.

Although the Treaty of Rome and the directives
only strictly require freedom of capital movement
within the Common Market, EEC has a bias in favor
of freedom of movement with the rest of the world.
In fact, Germany, Belgium, and Luxembourg impose
virtually no restrictions, and the other three do
not discriminate much between members and nonmem-
bers. Real problems may arise if membership is
broadened to include the United Kingdom and other
countries. [18] As explained above, the United Kingdom imposes rigid exchange control on capital movement anywhere outside the sterling area, including
notably Europe and North America. If Britain became a member of the EEC, restrictions on the purchase of European securities by United Kingdom
residents or on direct investment in Europe by
United Kingdom enterprises would have to be removed.
(There are, for practical purposes, no United Kingdom obstacles to inward movement.) Government
spokesmen appear to accept this position, but it is
generally assumed that a means will be found to
continue the present system of restrictions with
regard to investment elsewhere. (United Kingdom
investors have been traditionally enthusiastic and
successful buyers of U.S. and Canadian securities.)
The experience of other member states is not helpful; the Commission certainly takes the view that
exchange controls are self-defeating. It is hard
to see how United Kingdom residents can be given
freedom to invest without a premium in EEC securities, while at the same time being expected to
pay a 30 per cent premium to invest in the U.S.
How could they be prevented, for instance, from
buying a Euro-bond issue of a Luxembourg company
convertible into the stock of a U.S. parent or the
stock of EEC companies with substantial unrestricted investments in North America? Special situa-
tions will be set up very quickly to exploit any
gaps. Article 70, Paragraph 2, accepts but does
not solve the problem. There seems no really satisfactory solution. If the United Kingdom enters
the Common Market, this may pave the way for the
end of exchange control in the developed sterling
area. Such a step forward would leave the U.S.

isolated as the only developed country imposing restrictions on capital movements and deescalate the
game of "beggar my neighbor." With luck, it might
be possible for Europe to negotiate a form of General Agreement on Tariffs and Trade (GATT), covering capital movements, and persuade the U.S. to
remove the interest-equalization tax.

Belgium and Luxembourg

These countries impose no exchange-control restrictions affecting the Euro-bond market, although
certain transactions have to be made through the
free instead of the official market. This is a
technicality only, as the rates are virtually identical. A public issue of foreign securities is
subject to authorization from the appropriate finance ministry, and the rules of the relevant stock
exchanges must be complied with, but there is no
apparent discrimination against foreign securities.
(The convenience of the Luxembourg Stock Exchange
for international issues is well known and described
in more detail, in Chapter 2.)

France

France has traditionally taken a somewhat isolationist attitude to international finance. Since
January, 1959, the French franc has been convertible for nonresidents, but exchange control for
residents continued, subject only to the minimum
requirements of EEC (discussed above). A recent,
major liberalization measure, Law 66-1008, December 28, 1966, was widely hailed as an attempt to
reinstate Paris as a major international financial
center. This law virtually abolished exchange control for French residents, with a few exceptions
aimed mainly at limiting foreign investment in
France. Issues by foreigners on the French capital
market and borrowing abroad by French companies
still required specific consent. Direct investment
(defined as the acquisition of 20 per cent or more
of the capital of a company) still required permission, whether it was an investment abroad by French

capital or an investment in France by foreign capital.

Foreign companies were able to borrow on long term in France on the same terms as French residents. The intention was to open France to the Euro-bond market. There is a fairly effective system of regulating the flow of new bond issues that applies equally to domestic and foreign issues. Domestic borrowers had priority, and other things being equal, bond issues by foreign companies quoted on the Paris Bourse expected to receive more favorable treatment.

Germany

Germany is a creditor nation with no exchange-control restrictions as commonly understood. Encouragement is given to private investment in underdeveloped countries by a system of investment guarantees. For domestic monetary reasons, the German authorities like to keep interest rates at a higher level than those ruling in surrounding countries. Exchange control restrictions have as a rule ceased to be used to safeguard the balance of payments and seem nowadays intended mainly to ensure the autonomy of domestic monetary policies.

The main weapon used is the system of bank-liquidity ratios. In such countries as the United Kingdom, there are customary ratios--in the U.S., there are statutory ratios--as to the proportion of cash and other quick assets that must be held by banks. In Germany, a commercial bank must deposit with the Bundesbank a percentage of its own deposits, interest-free. For domestic deposits, the percentages are 14.3 per cent for demand deposits and 10 per cent for time deposits, but for foreign deposits, the rates are 30 per cent and 20 per cent, respectively. As most Euro-dollar loans are on a bank-to-bank basis, a German bank borrowing Euro-dollars at 4 per cent must deposit a fifth of this, free of interest, making the effective cost of the balance equivalent to 5 per cent. This arrangement amounts to an interest-equalization tax in reverse.

Direct loans by bond issues fall outside this
system. Interest on such securities once was payable gross to nonresidents, but the growth of the
international bond market made this leak important.
On March 23, 1964, it was announced that henceforth
a capital-yield tax of 25 per cent would be levied
on such interest except where prohibited by a double taxation agreement (see Chapter 5). As such
bonds are normally owned in tax havens, this too
has had the effect of an interest-equalization tax
in reverse. There are still a number of loopholes,
one of which has been the creation of German mutual
funds, specializing in investment of German bonds.
On present rules, no withholding tax is paid either
on the payment of interest of the bonds to the
funds or on distributions to shareholders in the
funds. Prospectuses are clearly marked "not available to foreign investors," but the issuers are
surely aware that the market for such bonds is the
foreign investor. It would be easy enough to block
this loophole, but the authorities seem to take the
view that some controlled leakage is acceptable.
Possibly it is understood that there is a level beyond which these activities would be subject to
amending legislation.

Germany still maintains Category D restrictions, in that credit balances of private nonresidents with German banks may not carry interest, and
domestic money-market paper may not be sold to nonresidents without permission. The combined effect
of these measures is not actually to restrict the
movement of capital in or out of Germany, but to
ensure that nonresidents cannot fully enjoy the
high interest rates ruling in Germany. German investors are correspondingly less likely to be attracted by overseas fixed-interest opportunities.
This situation has led several German companies
to make bond issues on the international market
through foreign subsidiaries. Unlike the British
and U.S. issues, where the aim has been to bypass
restrictions on the outflow of capital, German

companies have simply been seeking cheaper funds.
Siemens, for instance, issued a DM loan through a
Luxembourg subsidiary. The yield on this loan is
6.2 per cent, free of withholding tax. There is an
almost exactly comparable internal Siemens bond,
with approximately the same redemption date, and
exactly the same currency and security, which
yields 6.94 per cent before the 25 per cent withholding tax. Although this loan is stated to be
for the purposes of the group outside Germany,
there seems no reason in principle why a purely domestic German company should not raise cheap money
through a Luxembourg subsidiary and relend it to
the parent.

Italy

Italy still imposes restrictions on capital
movements within Category C. Specific permission
is required for an issue of securities by a foreign
company on an Italian market or an issue of securities of an Italian company on a foreign market.
Residents may deal freely in securities listed on
the markets of another EEC member state, but permission is required to invest in unlisted securities or to grant credit unconnected with commercial
transactions.

The Netherlands

As with Belgium, dealings in listed securities
are unrestricted, save that certain transactions
must take place through the Kroner account, free
market. This is not a practical obstacle. Permission is still needed for the purchase and sale of
unlisted securities and for certain types of commercial credit. The most important restriction
(to be removed under the third directive) is that
permission is still required for foreign issues on
the domestic capital market or the issue of Dutch
securities on foreign capital markets.

THE EUROPEAN FREE TRADE ASSOCIATION

The Treaty of Stockholm does not envisage economic integration and has no provision comparable to those in the Treaty of Rome regarding capital movements. Only two member countries, the United Kingdom and Switzerland, are international financial centers. (The United Kingdom is discussed above and Switzerland below.) The other member countries, Norway, Sweden, Denmark, Austria, and Portugal all have to a greater or lesser extent exchange-control restrictions on the flow of capital, specific consent being needed for the more important categories of international investment. This can usually be obtained for genuine commercial transactions. These restrictions have not influenced the shape or history of the Euro-bond market.

Sweden

In Sweden, specific authorization is required and usually granted for direct investment either abroad by nationals, or in Sweden by foreigners. Borrowing abroad for Swedish purposes is not usually permitted, but permission is usually obtainable for borrowings to finance non-Swedish subsidiaries or imports. Specific consent is needed to offer bond issues in Sweden on behalf of nonresidents, and such permission has normally only been granted for borrowers in other Scandinavian countries.

Residents may purchase foreign securities (or Swedish securities denominated in foreign currencies) from other residents without consent, but consent is needed for purchase from foreigners. This is normally only granted on a switching basis. Nonresidents wishing to buy Swedish securities must also normally deal in a switching market.

Switzerland

Switzerland imposes no exchange control, and has a strong and free currency, and has a banking system that is generally considered to be honest

and the most trustworthy in the world. Nevertheless, Switzerland has managed partly to isolate her
monetary system from that of the rest of the world,
and the country has certain limitations as an international financial center.

Under Article 8 of the Federal Banking Law of
November 8, 1934, restrictions can be imposed on
loans and credits to nonresidents. The banks must
receive prior authorization from the Swiss National
Bank for credits to nonresident borrowers exceeding
SF10 million, with a duration of one year or more.
Authorization is also required for bond issues in
excess of SF5 million. In practice, these restrictions have limited the role of the Swiss banks as
a source of capital into the international market.
Recently, the Swiss banks have been allowed to par-
ticipate in Euro-bond placings, provided that at
least half of their participation was placed outside Switzerland and that the Swiss portion was
placed without advertising.

Another limitation is the heavy capital duty
of 1.2 per cent on issues of bonds in Switzerland
for a period exceeding ten years, or pro rata for
shorter bonds. This limits the role of the Swiss
as underwriters, but certain banks have set up
underwriting subsidiaries outside Switzerland.

The Swiss National Bank has at present no
powers to impose liquidity requirements on banks.
As there is a limited money market, and the banks
never in practice need to use rediscount facilities, bank rate and open market operations are use-
less as instruments of control. Nevertheless, the
Bank succeeds in maintaining a tight control over
the banking system and enforcing an orderly queue
for new bond issues. There is limited scope for
foreign issuers to join the queue, but some have
been permitted.

Other regulations have from time to time prohibited the payment of interest on foreign deposits
in Swiss francs. This may be bypassed by accepting

deposits in another currency such as the U.S. dollar or by the Bank, as investment manager, placing its customer's funds in suitable investments, including non-Swiss money-market paper. The combined effects of these policies have been to keep Swiss interest rates below those of the rest of the world. The role of the Swiss Bank in the Euro-bond market has been much more important as custodian of funds available for investment than as dealer or underwriter.

NOTES TO CHAPTER 4

1. International Monetary Fund, Annual Report on Exchange Restrictions (Washington, D.C.: International Monetary Fund); Pick's Currency Yearbook (New York: Pick Publishing Corporation).

2. See, for instance, Les Investissements Americains en France (Paris: College des Science Sociales et Economiques); "Wir Kaufen die ganze Deutsche Industrie," Der Spiegel, No. 41 (1965); Bernd Muldan, "Should American Investment in the Common Market Be Condemned or Encouraged?" Intereconomies, No. 7 (1966).

3. Public Law 85-563, 1963; Amended by Public Law 89-243, 1965 (incorporated as Internal Revenue Code, Chapter 41, Section 4911, 4920[c]).

4. Public Law 9059, 1967.

5. Revenue Code, Section 4918.

6. Ibid., Section 4916.

7. Ibid., Section 4917.

8. Ibid., Section 4915 (c).

9. Ibid., Section 4915.

10.   Internal Revenue Code, Section 4918;
amended by Public Law 90-59.

11.   "The President's Balance-of-Payments Program," Crawley, No. 5616 (February 10, 1965); No.
5628 (March 5, 1965); No. 5633 (March 18, 1965).

12.   General consents are promulgated through
a series of "E.C. Notices." Unfortunately, these
are neither published nor confidential, but merely
circulate to authorized banks.
      This section is prepared with the aid of
these notices for various dates, supplemented by
"the oral tradition of the City of London." See
also Bank of England Quarterly (June, 1967).

13.   D. de M. Carey, "A Tax by Any Other Name,"
British Tax Review (June, 1967), p. 160.

14.   "Mutual Funds and Unit Trusts," C.O.,
Merriman F.C.A. (London: Pitman, 1965).

15.   Revised unofficial translation by the
United Kingdom Foreign Office, S.O. Code,
59-130-0-67 (London: Her Majesty's Stationery
Office, 1967).

16.   Journal Officel des Communautes Europeenes,
No. 43 (July 12, 1960), and No. 9 (January 22, 1963).

17.   European Economic Community, Proposition
Modifiée de Troisieme Directive pour la mise en
oeuvre de l'Article 67, COM(67)55, Addendum (February 7, 1967).

18.   John Chown, "Taxation, Exchange Control
and the Treaty of Rome," Investment Analyst (December, 1967).

CHAPTER 5 THE TAX TREATMENT OF INTEREST AND THE ROLE OF THE HOLDING COMPANY

BACKGROUND INFORMATION

In this chapter, we will consider the related topic of tax factors affecting the flow of interest payments between countries, the residence and corporate structure of the issuer, and the shape of the issue. Background information is given to explain the impact of taxation on the international bond market, but no attempt has been made to be comprehensive, nor is the information intended as a substitute for the advice of legal counsel.

Payments of interest may be taxed by withholding or otherwise in the country of origin and also by assessment in the country of the recipient's residence. The rate of withholding tax may be modified by double-tax agreements. For instance, issuers must in general deduct 30 per cent from interest payments to nonresidents, but no tax at all is withheld on payments to a long list of countries with which the U.S. has concluded double-tax agreements. Interest paid in these cases is generally taxable in the country of residence. Most countries that tax foreign-source income allow a credit for withholding taxes in any other country, and residents of such countries will normally be concerned only if the rate of withholding tax (if any) exceeds their personal or corporate rate. Whether the income is taxed in the country of origin or residence is in other cases a matter between governments.

The tax treatment of interest paid by borrowers in certain countries, including treaty modifications, as well as less-detailed summaries on the corresponding treatment of dividends are treated at the conclusion of this chapter.

Euro-bonds appeal chiefly to those who are exempt from tax for one reason or another. The market is therefore a market in net yields, and it is essential that interest be paid without withholding tax of any kind, regardless of the residence of the recipient. If the rate of interest on the international bond market is 6 per cent, a bond on which 20 per cent withholding tax were deducted would have to offer a gross yield of 7-1/2 per cent to be interesting to the market. In practice, such a gross yield might appeal more to local taxpayers, and such bonds would never be traded on the international bond market.

The problem facing the issuer is how to pay the tax-free return required by the borrower at the least cost to himself.

Governments and government agencies have no problem. If they want to borrow in the international bond market, they simply provide that interest will be paid without deduction of tax, whatever the general rules of the country may be. In the United Kingdom, for instance, bond interest is subject to withholding tax unless there is a treaty provision to the contrary. This rule applies to most government securities, but eight specific securities have been issued at various times that are free of all taxes when held by nonresidents. Although these are not international bonds as generally understood, they might compete for the same funds (currency considerations apart) as Euro-bonds. There is also no problem for private issuers in countries such as Denmark where withholding taxes are not levied on interest and where interest is allowed as a deduction in computing taxable corporate profits.

Where a parent company wishes to raise a loan to finance activities in a number of countries, tax problems will certainly arise. These are sometimes solved by raising the loan through a specially created holding company, perhaps in a country such as Luxembourg, where the group has no commercial activities at all.

The rest of this chapter is devoted to an analysis of corporate tax planning, illustrating the use of holding companies, and explaining the structure of certain recent issues.

The corporate borrower wishing to borrow on the Euro-bond market can choose between borrowing as a direct obligation of the parent company, as a direct obligation of a particular foreign operating subsidiary, or as an obligation of an intermediate international holding company.

THE ROLE OF THE SUBSIDIARY

We have found no examples to date of a true, public international issue by a "foreign operating subsidiary" solely for its own purposes in one country. The nearest example is the issue made by Deutsche Texaco (a Delaware company) to finance the acquisition of Erdol in Germany. Domestic bond issues by a subsidiary for its own purposes in one country are of course common enough.

As explained in Chapter 4, the U.S. parent seeking funds for foreign expansion outside the guidelines must create an obligation that would be subject to interest-equalization tax if bought by U.S. persons. There is, therefore, no question of a direct issue, and the choice is between an issue by a foreign corporation or a U.S. resident subsidiary deriving 80 per cent or more of its income from outside the U.S.

Parent companies in other countries have a choice between issuing international bonds as a

direct obligation or through a foreign subsidiary.
Of the issues listed in Table 12, ten European
companies (one United Kingdom, three German, three
Italian, and three Dutch), have raised loans
through Luxembourg subsidiaries. Companies in
Austria, Belgium, France, Finland, Germany, Italy,
the Netherlands, Norway, Japan, Portugal, South
Africa, Sweden, and the United Kingdom have made
direct issues. For such an issue to be recogniz-
able as an international loan, it must almost inevitably be in a currency other than that of the
issuing corporation's own country. For instance,
Companhia Uniao Fabril, a Portuguese company, made
a direct issue in European units of account and
specified that the loan was to be subject to Luxembourg law. That particular loan was for internal
use in Portugal.

Luxembourg is the almost universal choice of
those who choose to raise loans through an intermediate subsidiary. There are good reasons for
this, but other locations may have advantages for
certain purposes.

The advantage of an issue as a direct obligation of the parent company is that interest can
usually be deducted from the parent company's
profits. In the nature of things, the parent company is more likely to be earning profits at any
particular time than a subsidiary in any one country, especially during the initiation period, or
a period of expansion when tax holidays, investment-
tax credits, or accelerated depreciation are being
enjoyed. There may be exchange control disadvantages in direct issues by United Kingdom companies,
and the withholding-tax position is unsatisfactory
for Italian and German borrowers. A direct loan
by an operating subsidiary would have the advantage that interest would be directly deductible,
but it could be subject to withholding tax at
rates shown later in this chapter. It is also
convenient for an international group to raise a
number of separate loans on the market, and it may
be essential or at least desirable to raise a

single loan for the purpose of operations in several countries.

A U.S. parent wishing to carry on business within (and not just trade with) foreign countries can set up unincorporated branches or create locally registered subsidiaries in various countries. In either case, profits arising in each country will be subject to local taxes, generally the same taxes that are applied to domestically owned corporations. When dividends are distributed, there may be additional withholding taxes at rates that may vary with the country to which they are paid, whether they are paid to a holding company with a substantial interest or to a portfolio investor (discussed at the conclusion of this chapter). When the dividend is received in the U.S., it is subject to U.S. tax, less a credit for foreign tax. The sum received is grossed up to reflect the original pretax profits behind the dividend, and this gross sum then suffers U.S. tax with a full credit for tax already borne. Where overseas tax is in excess of the U.S. corporate rate (presently 48 per cent), there is in general no relief. There is, however, a provision by which U.S. corporations can opt for "over-all limitation" and can use the excess credits from a 60 per cent rate country against income otherwise taxable from a 30 per cent rate country, for example. (They can no longer marry up taxed dividends with interest exempt from local withholding taxes.) The treatment of branches is slightly different, in that the profits are taxable in the U.S. as they arise. In some countries, such branches pay only corporate tax and escape withholding tax. Other countries are not so generous. France, for instance, has rather complicated arrangements in an attempt to recapture dividend tax from the parent, while Germany and Belgium have a special rate for branch profits, designed to approximate the combined effect of corporate and withholding taxes.

Where the foreign tax rate is low (or where the local operation can take advantage of tax-sparing

arrangements ineffective for U.S. law), U.S. tax
may be deferred by accumulating profits in the
country of operation. For practical purposes, this
deferral may be indefinite as long as the operations continue, and it was once possible eventually to repatriate at capital-gains tax rates. This
is not always as advantageous as it might at first
seem. If the overseas rate of tax is 32 per cent,
there is a choice between accumulating 68 per cent
abroad or remitting and being left with 52 per cent
after U.S. tax and tax credit. If the 68 per cent
is subject to capital-gains tax, the U.S. parent
would have only 51 per cent on repatriation. The
possibilities of tax deferral have been substantially reduced by the U.S. Revenue Act of 1962,
but even before this there were at least two disadvantages. The country of operation may be a bad
political risk from which it is desirable to extract funds as soon as possible or permissible, or
the profits generated may be needed for expansion
elsewhere. The answer was often to interpose a
holding company in a low tax jurisdiction between
the parent and the operating subsidiaries. Funds
could then be transferred through the world without any U.S. taxation.

Holding companies of this kind were particularly singled out for attack by the Revenue Act
of 1962, but in any case the development of double
tax arrangements had made the structure less attractive. As Appendix B shows, rates of withholding tax on distributions to a tax-free base company
may be substantially higher than distribution direct to the U.S. Contrary to popular superstition,
the aggregate tax burden may be materially increased by arranging for foreign shareholdings to
be held in Panama, Bermuda, or some similar haven.

DOUBLE-TAX AGREEMENTS

Holding companies in such base countries often
created more tax problems than they solved. They
may, nevertheless, have substantial practicable and

administrative advantages and be essential for
joint ventures and international consortia. An alternative solution is the use of a holding company
in a country that does levy tax, that has double-
tax agreements with the countries in which operations take place, and that has a generous tax regi-
men to foreign source income. Three European
countries to be considered are Switzerland, the
Netherlands, and Luxembourg.

As the above statement may appear to conflict
with experience, we must explain that foreign-base
companies of other kinds may still offer very substantial advantages. One method is to divert
rather than to distribute profits to the base company. Dividends received by a holding company
have already borne corporate and withholding tax
in the country of source. In contrast, interest,
royalties, and management charges may be allowed
as a deduction against taxable profits in the
source country, in which case the only taxes payable are withholding taxes in the country of source
and tax chargeable in the base country. (The
treatment of interest is given later in this chapter.) Royalties receive similar treatment, and
reasonable management charges are often exempt.

By a careful choice of country and route, the
total tax charge can be kept very low. American
readers will be familiar with the old Curaçao route
for extracting income from the U.S. Curaçao enjoyed the extensive benefits of a U.S. and Netherlands double-tax agreement that provided inter alia
that interest and royalties were taxable only in
the country of receipt. Curaçao legislation provided (until recent amendments incited by U.S.
pressure) a maximum tax rate of 3 per cent on
foreign-source income (dividends, interest, and
royalties) of a holding company. Interest and
royalties arising in the U.S. that would suffer
30 per cent withholding tax if paid to Bermuda or
Panama suffered aggregate tax of only 3 per cent
by being routed through Curaçao. If the profits
had been taxable in the U.S. and paid to a Bermuda

resident as dividend, the total tax charge would
have been nearly 65 per cent. Many similar routes
are still open to divert profits from a wide range
of high-tax countries. Another method is the setting up of a sales organization in a low-tax country that can buy from an associated company in a
high-tax country, for resale on terms which leave
most of the profits in the low-tax base company.
Similar advantages may be obtained from the sale
of semifinished components. Governments are naturally tightening up revenue procedures and bringing in antiavoidance legislation to minimize the
abuse of such arrangements. The stricter U.S. attitude to Section 482 is but one example. There is
material for a whole book on this subject but one
that obviously will never be written. For present
purposes, it is sufficient to know that such techniques exist and that they involve what are loosely
described as foreign holding companies.

The withholding-tax disadvantages of a holding
company in a zero-tax country can be substantially
reduced by using holding companies in the Netherlands, Switzerland, and Luxembourg, as shown in
subsequent discussion.

AN EXAMINATION OF VARIOUS
NATIONAL PRACTICES

Switzerland

Switzerland (as shown later), has a useful
collection of double-tax agreements that substantially reduce withholding taxes on dividends and
interest paid to a Swiss company. Switzerland has,
therefore, been a popular location for holding companies. Swiss taxes are low, but not negligible.
Federal tax on income rises to 8 per cent. There
are also cantonal and communal taxes, but for most
purposes it is possible to pick a canton that
levies no tax on the income of holding companies.
As there are twenty-five cantons to choose from,
competition ensures that a suitable location can

generally be found. Both the federal government
and the cantons levy a capital tax on corporate
assets.

Dividends paid by a Swiss company are subject
to a 30 per cent withholding tax, reduced under
certain treaties. Interest paid is not subject to
withholding tax, and it was once possible to arrange for interest to be routed to Switzerland, to
claim the benefit of reduced rates of withholding
tax in the country of origin, and then from Switzerland to another country, such as Liechtenstein.
As interest paid balanced interest received, there
was no net taxable income in Switzerland. The
Swiss Government became embarrassed by the excessive use of this procedure, and the Federal Decree
of December 14, 1962, rendered foreign-controlled
companies ineligible for the advantage of Swiss
double-tax agreements, unless certain conditions
were met. Briefly, these conditions are:

1. Loans bearing interest must not exceed six
times the capital and reserves.

2. Not more than 50 per cent of the gross income from royalties, income, or dividends may be
paid for the benefit of persons not otherwise entitled to the advantages of a Swiss double-tax
agreement.

3. At least 25 per cent of the gross royalty,
interest, or dividend income derived from countries
with which Switzerland has a double-tax agreement
must be declared as a dividend by the Swiss company
(rendering the dividend liable to withholding tax
of 30 per cent generally).

If any of these requirements is not met, the
Swiss authorities will refuse to certify any claim
for exemption under a double-tax agreement.

It would be possible to use a Swiss company
as an intermediary for the purposes of raising an
international loan, but the company would not be

able to claim the benefit of the reduced rates of
withholding tax on its own receipts from various
countries unless its receipts from foreign sources
were at least double the interest it had to pay on
the loan. The balance of income accumulated might
be subject to 8 per cent federal tax, and there
would also be a capital tax of approximately 1/2
per cent, depending on the canton chosen. Switzerland is still a practical choice for a holding company to hold equity interests, where the owners of
the company are either resident of a country with
a double-tax agreement with Switzerland (such as
the U.S.) or investors living in a tax-haven country who plan to take their ultimate profit by the
capital-gains route.

The Netherlands

The general level of taxation in the Netherlands is high, but there are certain special priv-
ileges involving holding companies. These are of
two types, portfolio-investment companies and the
"Deelneeming" holding companies. The latter is
exempt from tax on dividends received in respect of
substantial participations in other companies, provided, in the case of foreign companies, that the
underlying profits have borne some tax (however low
the rate). The term "substantial participation" is
broadly defined, and a favorable ruling can usually
be obtained on borderline cases. Dividends received from such companies enjoy the benefits of
the reduced rates of withholding tax (shown later)
with no additional income tax in the Netherlands.
Following a recent amendment, gains on the realiza-
tion of such participations are exempt from capital-
gains tax. There is no capital tax in the Netherlands. At first sight, therefore, a Netherlands
holding company provides an excellent solution to
the problem.

An important limitation on their usefulness as
intermediary companies for international bond issues is that interest received by a Deelneeming
company does not enjoy any special exemption but is

taxed in the ordinary way as business income. Interest paid is allowed as a deduction, so that interest income can flow through without penalty. If
interest paid and received are identical, all is
well, but excess receipts are taxed in the Netherlands, while a shortfall might have to be made good
by bringing income into the company that had borne
tax in other countries.

Another problem may arise when the ultimate
parent wishes to realize the investment. Although
at present there is no withholding tax on dividends
paid to a U.S. stockholder, new legislation is expected imposing a general withholding tax of 25 per
cent. Treaties would then be renegotiated to provide for a reduction to 15 per cent. This penalty
may be enough to destroy the advantage, and under
Netherlands law, the withholding tax would also apply on any surplus arising on the liquidation of
the company.

The only example in Table 12 of a Netherlands
intermediate company being used as the issuers is
Queensland Alumina Holdings N.V. The equity of
this company is jointly owned by Kaiser (U.S.),
Alcan (Canada), Pechiney (France), and Conzinc Rio
Tinto (an Australian company controlled by a United
Kingdom company). This Netherlands company has
raised $20 million on the European market and has
applied the proceeds to the purchase of $20 million
debentures in Queensland Alumina Ltd., an Australian company. Queensland Alumina Ltd. borrowed a
further $30.6 million in the U.S. and Australia.
The prospectus explained that bauxite would be contributed to the smelter by the participants, pro
rata to their shareholdings. It also stated that
"it is expected that QAL will make a profit only
to the extent, if necessary, to permit it to use
an investment allowance [at] 20 per cent of the
cost of new plant and equipment under the Australian income tax law."

Luxembourg

The Luxembourg law of July 31, 1929, is specifically designed to provide a tax-neutral form of holding company. A holding company formed under this law that restricts its activities to investing in or lending to other companies is exempt from income taxes on its receipts and from withholding taxes on its dividends and interest payments. The only local tax possible is an annual tax on the capital (including loan capital) of 0.16 per cent. This makes the Luxembourg holding company the cheapest of the three possibilities considered. It is also the most straightforward, as the legislation has been specially designed to facilitate the transactions we are considering.

However, there is a major disadvantage. The double-tax agreements negotiated by Luxembourg exclude holding companies from the benefits of reduced rates of withholding tax. The Luxembourg route does not, therefore, save global taxes, and the result is exactly the same as if separate loans were made to each company. Luxembourg is not a particularly suitable location for the holding of equity participations. It is ideal for raising a loan on the Euro-bond market, provided that the sums raised are lent at interest to companies in other countries.

The solution, therefore, is for the parent company to hold its equity participations directly or through the Netherlands or Switzerland and to set up a separate Luxembourg company to raise money on the international market for relending to fellow subsidiaries. A recent example of this procedure was an issue by Siemens. Siemens already had a Swiss holding company to hold its foreign participations. A Luxembourg company, Siemens Europa Finanz A.G., was set up as a subsidiary of the Swiss holding company for the purpose of making a DM100 million issue at 7 per cent. To quote the prospectus: "The proceeds of this issue will be utilized to cover the financial requirements of

Siemens Group outside the Federal Republic of Germany." An interesting feature of this issue is that the borrower (as is usual) undertakes to pay any withholding taxes subsequently imposed but reserves the right to repay the bonds at 104, on ninety days' notice, should any such taxes be imposed.

The United States

The simplest procedure of the lot for the U.S. parent is to raise a loan through a U.S. company that derives 80 per cent or more of its income overseas. This company would pay U.S. corporate taxes in the normal way but could claim the benefits of the U.S. double-tax agreements and could claim interest as a deduction.

Special Problems of a United Kingdom Parent

United Kingdom companies have been surprisingly slow to take advantage of the international bond market in Europe. By 1968, only two had borrowed through a Luxembourg subsidiary, and four had made seven loans as direct obligations. More activity is now developing, notably the $50 million issue by Shell International Finance N.V., a Curaçao company jointly owned by Shell of the United Kingdom and Royal Dutch. As explained earlier, exchange-control factors might slightly favor the holding-company route, but direct investment is not ruled out as it is in the U.S., provided that the loan is made in a currency other than sterling.

Tax factors in the United Kingdom are similar to those in the U.S., full credit being granted against foreign tax paid. United Kingdom companies are not permitted to claim "over-all limitation" and pay the higher of United Kingdom or foreign tax on each particular source of income. On the other hand, relief is granted on underlying taxes no matter how long the chain of intermediary subsidiaries or how remote the source.

The most important distinction between the two
countries arises from the difference in rate structure. Although the corporation tax introduced by
the Labour Government in 1965 superficially re-
sembles the U.S. model, it is designed to be much
more discriminatory against both distributed profits and against foreign investment (both of which
are disliked by the Labour Government). The difference is that the rate of corporation tax on
profits is 40 per cent instead of 48 per cent,
while the rate of personal tax on dividends distributed is much higher than in the U.S. Tax rates
in most industrial countries are about 50 per cent,
which is near enough to the U.S. rate of corporation tax. Foreign-source income taxed at 50 per
cent received by a United Kingdom company would
have about 10 per cent of foreign tax unrelieved,
and in spite of eloquent arguments by industry and
the opposition, no permanent provision has yet been
made to allow this "over-spill" to be offset
against tax deducted from dividends. Although this
problem could in theory arise in the U.S., its
practical consequences are negligible, partly because of the difference in rates and partly because
of the possibility of over-all limitation. A practical consequence is that tax deferral through an
overseas holding company is much less often worthwhile for a United Kingdom parent.

Another special problem facing a United Kingdom based group is Section 468 of the Income Tax
Act of 1952. Under criminal penalties, this prohibits the transfer abroad of the whole or part of
the business of a United Kingdom company without
the consent of the Treasury. In 1957, some of the
worst anomalies of this clumsy section were relieved by legislation permitting companies to set
themselves up as overseas trade corporations, but
these provisions were repealed in 1965 as part of
the Labour Government's campaign against foreign
investment. The best hope now is that Section 468
will prove to be incompatible with the Treaty of
Rome if and when the United Kingdom joins the EEC.

Special Problems of Issuers
in Other Countries

As Table 12 shows, most issues by corporate borrowers have been direct loans to the parent company, the proceeds of which may have been lent to or invested in foreign subsidiaries. This procedure is not incompatible with the existence of intermediate foreign holding companies and, the loan raised may indeed be lent through such a company.

Germany normally grants credit relief as in the U.S. and the United Kingdom, but there are two useful special provisions. Some double-tax agreements (including that with the U.S.), exempt income arising in the other country from German taxation. As tax rates are usually comparable, the practical answer may be the same as that given by credit relief, but the arrangement is obviously administratively much simpler.

The other provision especially relevant to investment in underdeveloped countries is that companies have an option to pay tax at a special rate of 25 per cent on income actually received from overseas companies. This gives a materially better answer than credit relief, when overseas tax rates are low and administrative processes are simplified.

Several German companies have raised international issues through Luxembourg subsidiaries. The advantage of doing this is that it by-passes the 25 per cent coupon taxes levied on German bonds held by residents of countries with which there is no relevant treaty. As there is no withholding tax paid on certain other categories of interest, it may well be that the Luxembourg company in fact lends the money raised straight back to the parent. In the case of the Siemens DM issue (referred to above), this possibility was apparently excluded by the prospectus, and the group obviously had adequate non-German outlets for its funds.

France does not tax income arising overseas
and no special problem arises. As explained above,
Netherlands companies do not in practice suffer
Netherlands tax on income derived from overseas
operations.

Italy exempts dividends received from subsidiaries, but the exemption does not extend to income
earned through a foreign branch. Italian companies
frequently use holding companies in Switzerland to
handle their international activities. This does
not prevent the parent from raising money and lending it through the subsidiary.

Belgium has the most unsatisfactory rules of
any European country regarding relief from double
taxation on foreign-source income. In practice,
therefore, Belgian companies tend to conduct their
foreign operations through Swiss or other subsidiaries which are set up in such a way that they
never have to distribute income to Belgium. As
with Italy, a loan can be raised as principal and
re-lent to the foreign holding subsidiary.

A SUMMARY OF NATIONAL LAWS

The following comments summarize the main provisions of national law relating to the deduction
of tax from interest paid by a resident of one
country to a resident of another. Only the main
provisions are given. In particular, these rules
may not apply if the recipient has a permanent establishment in the country of residence of the
payer, or if the interest is paid otherwise than
at arms' length.

The United States

The general rule is that withholding tax at
the rate of 30 per cent must be deducted by the
payer from any interest paid to nonresidents. General exemptions (regardless of the residence of the
recipient) include:

1.   Bank-deposit interest not effectively connected with the U.S. trade or business of a nonresident.

2.   Interest paid by a U.S. corporation where
less than 20 per cent of income from all sources
has been derived from sources within the U.S. during the previous three years.   (U.S. Internal Revenue Code, Section 861[a][1][b].)   This is the exemption that makes possible the "Delaware" type of
Euro-bond issue.

Double-tax agreements with the following countries exempt the recipient from withholding taxes
on U.S. source interest: Austria, Denmark, Finland,
Germany, Greece, Ireland, Luxembourg, Netherlands,
Antilles, Norway, the United Kingdom, and most
British colonies actually imposing an income tax.
Agreements with Belgium, Canada, France, and Japan
reduce the rate of withholding tax from 30 per cent
to 15 per cent and the agreement with Switzerland
reduces the rate to 5 per cent.

The United Kingdom

The general rule is that "yearly interest of
money" (this term includes all bond interest), must
in general be paid after deduction of income tax
at the standard rate (now 41-1/4 per cent) if the
United Kingdom resident payer is to claim or effectively enjoy an offset in computing his own tax
liability.   Short interest on bank deposits for up
to 364 days is payable without deduction.   Interest
paid by a closely controlled company to shareholders and other connected persons, or the payment of
interest by a United Kingdom subsidiary to a nonresident parent, in general will be treated as a
distribution of profits, both subjected to income
tax and disallowed in computing profits subject to
corporation tax.

General exceptions consist of the following:

1.   A recent revenue ruling allows banks to

pay interest on deposits for over one year without
deduction of tax. This change was to facilitate
Euro-currency dealing.

2.   Certain British Government securities provide in the terms of their issue that the interest
is free of all United Kingdom taxes, present or
future, to nonresidents.

3.   Interest can be paid to a nonresident
without deduction of tax and be allowed as a charge
in computing taxable income, if the interest is incurred in connection with a trade carried on wholly
or mainly outside the United Kingdom, if the terms
of the contract provide for payment outside the
United Kingdom and if the interest is in fact so
paid to a nonresident. (Section 138 I.T.A. 1952,
extended to corporation tax by Section 52[5][b] F.A.
1965.)

Treaty exceptions for the United Kingdom include the following: double-tax agreements with
Germany, Greece, Ireland, Norway, Sweden, Switzerland, and the U.S. exempt interest paid to residents of those countries from withholding tax.

Companies in Austria, Denmark, Finland, Malawi,
Rhodesia, and Zambia receiving interest from United
Kingdom companies in which they also hold more than
half the voting shares suffer normal withholding
tax. Residents of Austria (again) and the Netherlands are taxed in the United Kingdom on interest
from loans secured on real property. In other
cases, residents of the countries named are exempt
from United Kingdom withholding tax on interest.

The 1965 tax changes in the United Kingdom are
not yet fully reflected in double-tax agreements.
For instance, the standard agreement with British
colonies does not exempt interest but does, by interpretation, exempt dividends from withholding
tax. It seems possible that most revised agreements will follow the U.S. precedent and nullify
the provision that interest paid to a nonresident

parent is not allowed as a deduction for corporation tax purposes.

France

The tax treatment of interest was materially
changed in 1966. The "Prelevement" withholding tax
of 25 per cent is now levied on most interest payments. In certain circumstances, residents can
treat this as an optional final tax in lieu of income taxes. A number of administrative instruc-
tions have been issued purporting to clear up the
operation of this tax, but the position must still
be regarded as subject to further amendments. The
position of taxpayers having an establishment or
some residential status both in France and elsewhere is in particular need of clarification.

The general rule now is that interest paid by
a French company or branch of a foreign company to
a nonresident is subject to withholding tax of 25
per cent.

General exemptions include:

1.   Interest on savings-bank deposits and on
certain government and government-guaranteed securities.

2.   Interest on foreign currency deposits with
French banks.

3.   Interest on short-term (up to two years)
interbank operations.

4.   Interest on bonds issued abroad by French
companies in respect of which the prior approval of
the French Ministry of Finance has been obtained.
(Such approval would be vital for a true Euro-bond.)

Treaty exceptions for France are also varied.
Certain double-tax agreements provide for reduced
rates of withholding tax. Most of these were
signed prior to the new legislation. To prevent

anomalies, it has now been provided unilaterally
that where there is an effective double-tax agreement, the rate of withholding tax will not exceed
12 per cent in the case of negotiable bonds issued
before January 1, 1965, and 10 per cent in other
cases. This provision appears to apply to interest
payments for residents of Belgium, Greece, Israel,
Luxembourg, Monaco, Spain, the United Kingdom, the
U.S., and to the territories of the former French
community.

Because of existing, more favorable treaty
provisions, interest paid to residents of the following countries is exempt from withholding tax:
Austria, Denmark, Finland, Germany, Lebanon, the
Netherlands, Norway, Sweden, and Switzerland.
Japanese residents are subject to a maximum of 10
per cent, with complete exemption in certain cases.
It may be expected that these provisions will be
amended when the treaties come up for renegotiation.

Austria

In general, no withholding tax is levied on
interest paid to nonresidents. There are two main
exceptions. Interest on convertible and profit-
sharing bonds is treated in the same way as dividends (discussed later). Interest on loans secured
to real property in Austria is taxed as if it were
business income of a branch in Austria.

Belgium

Interest is subject to a withholding tax of
20 per cent, reduced to 15 per cent by treaties
with Finland, France, and the U.S.

Denmark

Interest paid to nonresidents not having a
permanent establishment in Denmark is not at present subject to withholding tax. Provisions intro-
ducing withholding tax are expected to be introduced shortly.

Finland

In general, no withholding tax is levied on bond and bank interest. Interest on profit-sharing bonds is subject to 30 per cent withholding tax, waived by agreements with Austria, Denmark, France, Germany, the Netherlands, Sweden, Switzerland, and the U.S. Withholding tax is reduced to 15 per cent on payments to Belgium and Canada.

Germany

Bond interest paid to nonresidents is subject to 25 per cent withholding tax, imposed since June 28, 1965. This particular tax is of more general significance for the Euro-bond market and is fully discussed earlier. Residents of Austria, Denmark, France, the Netherlands, Norway, Sweden, and the U.S. can claim a full refund of this withholding tax. The effective rate for residents of Canada and Luxembourg (other than holding companies), is 15 per cent. Residents of the United Kingdom and the Republic of Ireland also enjoy the 15 per cent rate, unless the recipient owns 25 per cent or more of the equity of the German paying company. Residents of Switzerland are exempt except in respect of convertible or profit-sharing bonds, of which 15 per cent is withheld.

Interest on loans secured by German real property is taxed as business income derived through a permanent establishment in Germany. Bank and other interest is not subject to withholding tax, but a similar result is achieved by differential system of Bundesbank deposits.

Greece

Bank deposits, interest, and government loans are free of withholding tax. Other interest paid to nonresidents is taxed as business income, at a standard rate of 40-1/4 per cent.

Ireland

The general law follows that the United Kingdom income tax at the standard rate of 35 per cent is deducted or withheld on annual interest paid to nonresidents. This is waived by treaties with Denmark, Germany, and the United Kingdom, and on payments to the U.S. except where the recipient controls more than 50 per cent of the voting power of the Irish company.

Italy

Interest paid to nonresidents is subject to 27 per cent tax on income from movable capital, increased by municipal and other surcharges. The effective rate was generally about 32.4 per cent, increased to about 36 per cent by the 10 per cent temporary surcharge enacted for 1967 and subsequent years. This withholding tax is waived by treaties with Austria and Germany.

Luxembourg

Interest paid by holding companies is exempt from withholding tax regardless of the residence of the recipient (discussed earlier). Holding companies cannot claim the benefit of double-tax agreements in respect of interest received by them from outside the country.

In the case of ordinary trading companies operating in Luxembourg, the general rule is that interest on convertible or profit-sharing bonds is subject to a 15 per cent withholding tax, while interest on other bonds is subject to 5 per cent. Bank and other interest is exempt. Interest on loans secured by Luxembourg real property is subject to tax as business income at the rate of 40 per cent on income and 1/2 per cent on net worth. Interest payments to Austrian residents are exempt. Bond interest paid to U.S. residents is exempt, but real property loans are taxed in accordance with the general rule.

The Netherlands

Interest payments are not subject to withholding tax, except that profit-sharing bonds suffer withholding tax of 25 per cent, and interest on loans secured on Netherlands real property is taxed as business income. Both categories are exempt by treaties with Denmark, France, Norway, Sweden, and the U.S. Treaties with Finland, Italy, Portugal, and the United Kingdom exempt profit-sharing bonds but not income from real property.

Norway

No withholding tax is deducted on bond or other interest paid to nonresidents. Some double-tax treaties limit Norway's freedom of action to withhold tax in the future.

Portugal

Bond interest is subject to an 8 per cent tax, plus local surcharges on income from movable capital, plus a 5 per cent substitute-inheritance tax. There is also an 0.05 per cent substitute-stamp tax withheld annually on the market value of the bonds. Other interest is subject to withholding tax of 15 per cent plus local surcharges. The local surcharges may be up to 12 per cent of tax otherwise due. There are no treaty reductions or exemptions.

Spain

Interest paid to nonresidents is subject to a 2.5 per cent turnover tax and a 24 per cent withholding tax. The withholding tax is reduced to 10 per cent when paid to residents of Norway, Sweden, and Switzerland.

Sweden

No withholding tax is deducted on bond or other interest paid to nonresidents. Some double-tax treaties limit Sweden's freedom of action to withhold tax in the future.

Switzerland

Interest on bond and bank deposits is subject to a 30 per cent federal withholding tax. The definition of income liable is somewhat broader than usual. This withholding tax is waived on payments to residents of Austria, Finland, Germany, and the United Kingdom; reduced to 5 per cent on payments to residents of the Netherlands, Norway, Sweden, and the U.S.; and to 10 per cent on payments to residents of Denmark, France, and Spain. Interest on loans secured by Swiss real property is taxed as business income, with certain treaty reductions and exemptions. The limited categories of interest not covered by these definitions are free of withholding tax. There are no cantonal or communal withholding taxes on interest.

WITHHOLDING TAXES ON INTERNATIONAL DIVIDENDS

Withholding taxes deducted from dividends in the country of source may depend on the degree of relationship between the paying and receiving company, and on whether or not there is an effective double-tax agreement between the countries. Table 8 deals with dividends on portfolio securities, while Table 9 indicates amendments where the receiving company holds a substantial participation in the paying company.

These tables are by no means comprehensive. They show the effect on double-tax agreements only with the United Kingdom, the U.S., and the three countries discussed in the text as possible locations for holding companies. Reduced rates of withholding tax do not necessarily apply if the recipient has a permanent establishment in the country of residence of the paying company or is controlled by residents of the latter country.

TABLE 8

Withholding-Tax Rates on Portfolio Dividends

Paying Country	General Rule (no treaty)	Luxembourg[a] (nonholding)	The Netherlands	Switzerland	United Kingdom	United States
Austria	18.15	15.00	18.15	Nil	18.15	9.075
Belgium	20.00	20.00	20.00	20.00	20.00	15.00-18.2[b]
Denmark	Nil	Nil	Nil	Nil	Nil	Nil
Finland	47.00	47.00	10.00	5.00	5.00	15.00
France	25.00	25.00	Nil	15.00	25.00	15.00
Germany	25.00	15.00	15.00	15.00	15.00	15.00
Greece	42.05	42.05	42.05	42.05	42.05	42.05
Ireland	35.00	35.00	35.00	35.00	Nil	35.00
Italy	30.00	30.00	30.00	30.00	Nil	15.00
Luxembourg[a]	15.00	--	15.00	15.00	15.00	7.50
The Netherlands	25.00	25.00	--	15.00	Nil	15.00

Norway	25.00	25.00	10.00	5.00	5.00	15.00
Portugal[c]	--	--	--	--	--	--
Spain	15.00	15.00	15.00	15.00	15.00	15.00
Sweden	30.00	30.00	10.00	5.00	Nil	15.00
Switzerland	30.00	30.00	15.00	--	15.00	15.00
United Kingdom	41.25	41.25	Nil	15.00	--	15.00
United States	30.00	15.00	15.00	15.00	15.00	--

[a] Dividends paid by Luxembourg holding companies are exempt from withholding tax. Dividends paid to Luxembourg holding companies are not eligible for treaty-reduced rates and suffer with- holding tax in the country of origin under the general rule.

[b] Dividends paid by a Belgian company to a U.S. shareholder have tax withheld at 15 per cent, provided that the shares have been held in registered form for twelve months prior to the payment of the dividend or since issue. In other cases, the 18.2 per cent rate applies.

[c] The tax treatment of dividends paid by Portuguese companies is complicated and largely irrelevant. The treatment is not affected by any double-tax agreement.

Source: Taxation of Patent Royalties, Dividends and Interest in Europe (looseleaf service) (Amsterdam: International Bureau of Fiscal Documentation).

TABLE 9

Withholding-Tax Rates on Dividends Paid to Stockholders with Substantial Participation

Paying Country	General Rule (no treaty)	Luxembourg[a] (nonholding)	The Netherlands	Switzerland	United Kingdom	United States
Austria	18.95	5.00 (25.00)	18.15	Nil	10.00 (50.00)	5.00 (95.00)
Belgium	20.00	20.00	20.00	20.00	20.00	15.00–18.2[b]
Denmark	Nil	Nil	Nil	Nil	Nil	Nil
Finland	47.00	47.00	Nil (50.00)	5.00	Nil (50.00)	5.00 (95.00)
France	25.00	25.00	Nil	15.00	10.00 (50.00)	15.00
Germany[d]	25.00 (25.00)	25.00 (25.00)	25.00 (25.00)	25.00 (25.00)	25.00 (25.00)	15.00–25.00[e]
Greece	42.05	42.05	42.05	42.05	42.05	42.05
Ireland	35.00	35.00	35.00	35.00	Nil	35.00
Italy	30.00	30.00	30.00	Nil	5.00 (95.00)	--
Luxembourg[a]	15.00	--	15.00	15.00	15.00	5.00/7.50[f]
The Netherlands	25.00	25.00	--	Nil (25.00)	Nil	5.00 (25.00)
Norway	25.00	25.00	Nil (50.00)	5.00	Nil (50.00)	5.00 (50.00)
Portugal[c]	--	--	--	--	--	--
Spain	15.00	15.00	15.00	10.00 (25.00)	15.00	15.00

Sweden	30.00	30.00	Nil (50.00)	5.00	Nil	5.00 (50.00)
Switzerland	30.00	30.00	Nil (25.00)	--	5.00 (25.00)	5.00 (95.00)
United Kingdom	41.25	41.25	Nil	5.00 (25.00)	--	15.00
United States	30.00	15.00	15.00	15.00	15.00	--

Note: Numbers in parentheses indicate the minimum percentage constituting a substantial participation. Where there is no figure, no distinction is made.

aDividends paid by Luxembourg holding companies are exempt from withholding tax. Dividends paid
to Luxembourg holding companies are not eligible for treaty-reduced rates and suffer withholding tax
in the country of origin under the general rule.

bDividends paid by a Belgian company to a U.S. shareholder have tax withheld at 15 per cent,
provided that the shares have been held in registered form for twelve months prior to the payment
of the dividend or since issue. In other cases, the 18.2 per cent rate applies.

cThe tax treatment of dividends paid by Portuguese companies is complicated and largely irrelevant. The treatment is not affected by any double-tax agreement.

dIn Germany, the reduced treaty rates of withholding tax apply only if the receiving company
owns less than 25 per cent of the shares of the German paying company.

eA U.S. company owning 10 per cent or more of the shares of a German company can claim the
benefit of the 15 per cent rate of withholding tax, unless a material part of the dividend is
reinvested or lent to the paying company.

fThe 5 per cent rate applies if 50 per cent or more of the Luxembourg company is held by one
to four U.S. corporations, each of which individually owns at least 10 per cent.

Source: Taxation of Patent Royalties, Dividends and Interest in Europe (looseleaf service)
(Amsterdam: International Bureau of Fiscal Documentation).

NOTES TO CHAPTER 5

The material in this chapter has been drawn
from looseleaf legislation sources for various
countries, such as The Federal Tax Guide, Commerce
Clearing House, British Tax Encyclopedia, Sweet and
Maxwell, and other professional sources. The general reader seeking more detailed information on
tax legislation of various countries might refer to
the appropriate volumes of the World Tax Series,
published by Commerce Clearing House, Inc., for
Harvard Law School. These cannot be used profes-
sionally, as they inevitably will not reflect the
latest information. The special publication, Tax
Factors in Basing International Business Abroad
(Commerce Clearing House, 1957), is still an excellent introduction in spite of its age.

Executives of borrowing corporations and investment houses who require more detailed knowledge
and who can recognize the point at which professional advice should be sought are referred to:

Business International (weekly) (New York: Busi-
     ness International Corporation).

European Taxation (monthly), and Supplementary Ser-
     vice (Amsterdam: International Bureau of Fis-
     cal Documentation).

Investment, Licensing and Trading Conditions Abroad
     (New York: Business International Corporation).

Taxation of Patent Royalties, Dividends and Interest
     in Europe (looseleaf service) (Amsterdam:
     International Bureau of Fiscal Documentation).

Taxation of Private Investors in Europe (a new
     looseleaf service) (Amsterdam: International
     Bureau of Fiscal Documentation).

6

INTRODUCTION

Thus far, we have dealt with the practical operations of the Euro-bond market, and with a description of the legal, institutional, and tax factors that have stimulated its creation and helped determine its shape. We will now briefly consider the economic implications of the market.

Is it true, for instance, that the large volume of U. S. borrowing in Europe has pushed European interest rates up, or would they have risen in any case for other reasons? What effect has the market had on the U.S. balance of payments, on the dollar, on international interest rates, on international liquidity, and on the optimum employment of scarce capital resources? These are but some of the questions; for most of which there are no clear and undisputed answers. The relevant statistics are often not available, and even when they are, experts often disagree on their interpretation.

Although the authors are economists by training, we are principally concerned in our day-to-day work with the practical operation of financial markets. Others in universities and elsewhere are in a better position to undertake rigorous economic analyses, and it is hoped that this work will provide them with some of the facts they need.

However, our concerns here are an attempt at
analysis, partly to give the academic reader a
starting point for his arguments, but mainly to
provide dealers, underwriters, borrowers, and investors with some insight into the range of questions raised by the creation of any new financial
market.

It is essential to consider not only the real
benefits and dangers of the market, but the
imagined effects may also be important. Governments take views on the effects of certain types of
international financial operations in their domestic economies, and in one sense, it does not matter
whether their views are right or wrong. If they
hold certain views (and cannot be convinced that
they are in error), they will act on them. In
Chapter 4 and Chapter 5, we have shown that government actions (rational or not) have played a leading role in the history of the market thus far.
Future actions of governments may well change the
course of the market and that subject is discussed
in Chapter 7.

We will begin here with a short discussion on
the separate but related issue of the Euro-dollar
market, and go on to consider four main topics:
the effect of the market on the balance of payments (in the U.S. and elsewhere), on exchange
rates (spot and forward), on domestic interest
rates, and on the optimum allocation of capital
resources. This last topic is, after all, one
aspect of the central subject matter of economics
as a science.

THE EURO-DOLLAR MARKET

The term "Euro-bond" is obviously an abbrevi-
ation of "Euro-dollar Bond." Indeed, Euro-bonds
are often inaccurately thought of as international
bonds subscribed for with Euro-dollars. The two
phenomena and the two markets are logically dis-
tinct. The international bond market could have

grown up without the prior invention of the Euro-
dollar. The mere existence of a short-term Euro-
dollar market would not itself have led to the
development of the longer-term Euro-bond market, if
the other factors already discussed in this book
had not been present. Nevertheless, the two phe-
noma are related and may be thought of as the short
and long end respectively of an international capital market.

Definition of the Euro-dollar

What is a Euro-dollar? The answer to this
question is either complex and elusive or very
simple. The _Economist_ called it "one of those
jargon words."[1] The simple definition that we
prefer is: A Euro-dollar is a U.S. dollar deposited in a bank outside the U.S., which is not
necessarily a European bank. The owners of the
dollars can be U.S. citizens or corporations, a
Swiss industrialist, a South American rancher, a
Middle East oil king, or almost any other individual
or group. It does not matter who the owner is.
What does matter is that the dollars are deposited
or redeposited outside the U.S. and can therefore
be regarded as part of U.S. liquid liabilities
available to foreigners. Except to the extent to
which Euro-dollar balances are used for the creation of dollar credit by pyramiding, the original
dollars remain in the U.S.[2]

Another major point is that Euro-dollars are
no different from ordinary dollars, except in
their location. This is made very clear by Paul
Einzig:

> Eurodollars are not a special type of
> dollars and there is nothing to dis-
> tinguish them from ordinary dollars
> beyond the fact that they have been
> redeposited with a foreign bank. This
> may sound like stating the obvious.
> Yet it is very frequently overlooked.
> A great many people imagine that

> eurodollars are a special category
> of dollars somewhat similar to the
> various types of sterling after the
> war. All such special types of
> currencies had separate exchange
> rates because there were differences
> between the ways in which their
> holders were entitled to use them.
> On the other hand dollars redeposited
> in Europe remain with banks in the
> U.S. They are interchangeable with
> ordinary dollars and there is of
> course no separate exchange rate (as
> distinct from interest rate) for
> eurodollars.[3]

The final distinction is important. While Euro-dollars are indistinguishable from ordinary dollars in many respects, they have an entirely separate interest-rate structure, divorced from domestic restrictions and dependent on international supply and demand. It is indeed mainly because of certain restrictions that the market has come into being. The interest-equalization tax and Regulation Q, as well as traditions limiting banking flexibility in various countries, are the main reasons that London or Paris should offer a different interest-rate structure from New York for the same currency.

Funds in the Euro-dollar market come from the U.S. and from other countries, and some of the deposits are owned by central banks and other monetary institutions. Demand comes from countries all over the world, including the U.S. and the U.S.S.R. Funds may be employed as dollars or switched into the required domestic currency with or without forward-exchange cover.

Examples of the Euro-dollar Market

The owner of a currency balance (in U.S. dollars, for example), who wants to invest it for three months, can accept the rate of interest

offered for a dollar deposit for this period.
Alternatively, he can make a deposit in another
currency such as sterling, purchasing the currency
in the spot market and entering into a forward
contract to sell sterling for dollars in three
months' time at a predetermined price. The spot
and forward rates will usually differ, and the
sterling rate of interest for three month deposit,
adjusted for the cost of cover, effectively gives
an alternative rate of interest to a dollar de-
positor who is completely covered (or hedged)
against fluctuations in the exchange rate. Einzig[4]
discusses the fascinating implications of covered
arbitrage on exchange rates, interest rates, and
the balance of payments at length.

The following example illustrates the basic
problems: On April 26, 1967, the rate of interest
offered on three month Euro-dollar deposits was
4-3/4 per cent. United Kingdom local authorities
(municipalities) were offering 5-7/8 per cent for
three months on sterling deposits. The spot rate
of exchange was £1 = $2.7994; the three month
forward rate was $2.7920. A dollar owner who
bought spot sterling and simultaneously contracted
to sell three months' hence would lose 17/64 per
cent on the difference between the two rates over
the period, making the "cost of forward cover"
equivalent to 1-1/16 per cent per annum. This
reduces the effective dollar return from the
sterling deposit to 4-13/16 per cent, (5-7/8 per
cent - 1-1/16 per cent). This is better than the
Euro-dollar rate of 4-3/4 per cent. In technical
language, "the covered arbitrage margin was
1/16 per cent in favor of London."

The interest arbitrage position reveals a
great deal about the flow of international funds
and is a figure watched carefully by those concerned with the health of a currency. The traditional comparison between the United Kingdom and
the United States was based on rates for three
months on the treasury bills of the two countries,
but this has now ceased to have much meaning. In

our example, the April 26 figure on this basis
was 9/16 per cent in favor of London--a level
indicating that the holders of U.S. treasuries do
not regard covered arbitrage as an available
alternative. It is clear that internationally
mobile short-term funds now regard Euro-dollars
and United Kingdom local authority deposits as
the best investments in the respective currencies,
and arbitrage keeps the rates of interest (allow-
ing for cover) very close.

Perhaps the most significant (but often over-
looked) feature of the Euro-dollar market is the
extent to which a genuine wholesale market in
deposits has been created. The minimum transaction is normally $1 million. If a German bank
wishes to lend money to a French bank, the deposit
is now usually in Euro-dollars (i.e., in the currency of neither), and the two banks will make
their own foreign-exchange dispositions according
to the source from which they obtained the funds
or the use to which they are to be put. This
procedure achieves nothing that in principle could
not be achieved equally well by the old procedure,
where the lender made the deposit in the recipient
bank's currency and covered his currency risk in
the forward market. In practice, dealing has been
simplified by the adoption of one currency, and
therefore, one interest-rate structure for many
wholesale transactions, and dealing margins have
become very fine indeed. It is also interesting
to note that a side effect of the growth of the
market has been to transfer responsibility for
much interbank lending from the money departments
of banks to their foreign-exchange departments.
The real changes may have been procedural rather
than economic.

The Euro-dollar market is thus a true international money market, and involves some $13 bil-
lion. It is a phenomenon separate from the Euro-
bond market, and either could exist without the
other. The two do in practice relate, with the
Euro-bond market as the longer end of an

international capital market. Banks employ Euro-
dollar deposits to finance inventories of Euro-
bonds in the course of placing issues. Euro-bond
issues are often made, at least in part, to fund
existing Euro-dollar borrowings, or the proceeds
are deposited as Euro-dollars until they are required for the purpose of which the issue was
made. Either way, part of the proceeds of the issue of Euro-bonds will flow back into the Euro-
dollar market, at least temporarily. At the same
time, the issue may absorb Euro-dollar deposits
held by investors awaiting a suitable longer-term
home for their money.

THE EURO-BOND MARKET

Has the growth of the Euro-bond market increased or decreased the volume of Euro-dollar
deposits, and how, if at all, are international
short-term rates related to Euro-bond rates? There
are no simple answers to these questions. The
market provides both borrowers and investors with
a wider range of choice, and there is insufficient
evidence thus far as to whether the Euro-bond
market absorbs or releases Euro-dollars on balance.
The activities of issuing houses and underwriters
in Euro-bond operations are likely to have produced a once-and-for-all increase in the demand
for Euro-dollars to finance inventories that will
continue proportionate to the volume of new issues.

We are not suggesting that Euro-dollars provide long-term financing for Euro-bonds. This
would be surprising and bad banking practice.
Sophisticated investors will know from first
principles, and others should have learned the
perils of borrowing short and lending long from
recently wide fluctuations of interest rates.

On the other hand, it is possible that Euro-
bond borrowing presents an alternative to Euro-
dollar borrowing, especially if the formers' interest rates are low. And this will tend to

reduce the demand for Euro-dollars. More im-
portantly, it is possible that Euro-bond proceeds
will be used to repay prior Euro-dollar loans, or
indeed, will be employed in the market at least
temporarily. Therefore, the key question is
whether the impact of Euro-bonds or Euro-dollars
is mainly via reducing demand for the latter (by
providing an alternative long-term source of
funds), or whether, in fact, demand for Euro-
dollars increases for short-term financing, and
the pool is further depleted via consolidation.

On balance, the operation of the Euro-bond
market seems likely to expand the Euro-dollar
market, but this is only a personal judgment and
is not based on hard evidence. Statistics are
difficult to come by, but it appears that in
eighteen months prior to June, 1966, U.S. corporations borrowed $530 million through affiliates
but employed only $157 million in direct invest-
ment outside the U.S. If these figures (derived
from various sources) are correct or at least
comparable, the presumption must be that the difference was either deposited in the Euro-dollar
market pending the progress of investment plans
or that the borrowings were used to repay existing
Euro-dollar loans. To a large extent, the issues
may have been funding operations; other things
being equal (which they never are) the rise of
Euro-dollar interest rates would then have been
depressed or checked. This effect could be can-
celled out or even reversed if the issues had been
subscribed largely with short-term Euro-dollar
deposits.

THE U.S. BALANCE OF PAYMENTS

What has been the effect of the growth of
the international bond market on the U.S. balance
of payments? As discussed in Chapter 4, the
market has been given much of its impetus by
measures designed to protect the balance of payments. The interest-equalization tax closed the

U.S. market to some foreign borrowers, and the
voluntary guidelines deliberately incited U.S.
corporations to borrow abroad for expansion
abroad. The market has helped the U.S. to check
the outflow of capital without unduly inhibiting
the international operations of her corporations.
It would seem that the effect on the balance of
payments must have been beneficial, as the market
has made tolerably acceptable restrictions that
would otherwise have been resisted much more
strongly by business. Reality is never quite as
simple. First of all, any form of exchange control or restriction on capital movements inevitably creates its own anomalies, leaks, and loopholes, such as the widespread evasion of the
interest-equalization tax discussed earlier. Such
evasions may merely limit the effectiveness of the
restrictions, but in other cases they may draw
attention to the situation and lead to a larger
outflow than there would otherwise have been.
After all, no one wants to escape unless someone
else puts up a wall, and people who see a wall may
think of themselves as prisoners and may want to
jump over it. This is certainly the view that is
now taken of exchange control by European banking
experts. As long as there is no control, people
keep their money at home. As soon as control is
imposed, everyone seeks opportunities to transfer
money abroad for possible future emergencies. If
France or the Netherlands were for some reason to
reimpose exchange control, there would be an
enormous flight of capital through all of the inevitable chinks in the armor. The long-suffering
British are still usually law-abiding from long
habit, but they too are learning.

Apart from the perverse effect on equities,
the U.S. tax has been successful in closing its
new issue market to nonresident borrowers for
bonds of certain types. It has certainly enabled
the U.S. to pursue a policy of keeping interest
rates below world-market levels. The wisdom of
this policy is questionable, but it is perhaps inevitable in a country where interest rates are a
major issue with the agrarian vote.

The voluntary guidelines have been effective, mainly because they <u>are</u> voluntary and directed to the larger corporations. Sensibly, the smaller corporations that would have difficulty in raising an international bond issue have not been called upon to take part in the voluntary program. This has eliminated one objection to restrictions as imposed in the United Kingdom which hits particularly hard on the new company with no foreign investment record. The U.S. scheme leaves sufficient flexibility for the newcomer with an idea to get it off the ground and preserves the adaptability of financial institutions.

It does not follow, if a U.S. corporation makes a $10 million bond issue in Europe to finance expansion that might otherwise be financed in the U.S., that there is a corresponding net benefit in the U.S. balance of payments. The Bank for International Settlements[5] has estimated that about one third of the funds invested in Euro-bonds were obtained by the sale of U.S. investments by foreigners. If this is correct, the balance-of-payments benefit represents two thirds of the Euro-bond issues made to finance investments that would otherwise have been financed from U.S. sources. But some projects financed by Euro-bonds would have been canceled or postponed if the market did not exist, and one third of the cost of this would fall as a net loss to the balance of payments. Much the same applies to borrowings by other than U.S. issuers, especially if these are not merely a substitute for domestic issues.

To analyze the net effect, we need more information. What other leaks are there? Do U.S. funds leak out, legally or otherwise, to finance the purchase of Euro-bonds? Average figures can be very misleading. What is the effect of a marginal increase in Euro-bond borrowing on the sale of European-owned U.S. securities and on the leak of U.S. funds into the market? To what extent have U.S. corporations been making issues in

anticipation of future needs and perhaps in fear
of new restrictions or congestion in the market?
If they are doing this, what are the secondary
effects of the surplus funds released into the
Euro-dollar market? Probably the net effect on
the U.S. balance of payments will prove to be
substantially positive, mainly because of the
success of the market in harnessing previously untapped sources of funds for long-term investment.

An additional point is that individuals and
corporations invest to make money. If the U.S.
refuses to allow its reserves to be invested
abroad, it foregoes the potential return on this
investment. This is not to dismiss the need for
restrictions. A country, particularly a reserve-
currency country, is rather like a bank, and any
bank must frequently forego profitable investment
opportunities in the interests of liquidity and to
ensure confidence and survival. To the extent to
which corporations raise money in the Euro-bond
market by straight bond issues, there is an extra
interest cost of more than 1 per cent per annum.
This cost is borne both by the company and (indirectly) by the country's reserves. The government recognizes this position, and corporations
have been explicitly asked to bear this extra
burden as part of their contribution to the balance-of-payments program. Where convertible bonds
are issued, the position is more complicated. If
the parent corporation does well, nonresidents
will convert their bonds and sell the resulting
stocks to U.S. investors, neutralizing any balance-
of-payment benefit. If the stocks had been sold
to U.S. investors to finance the project in the
first place, the profit on the increase in value
of the stocks would have gone to U.S. residents
(and reserves) rather than to foreigners.

THE U.K. BALANCE OF PAYMENTS

Sterling area investors subject to the dollar
premium are unlikely to buy Euro-bond issues as

income investments. Convertibles can occasionally
be attractive. Euro-bond borrowing by U.K. companies must help the United Kingdom balance of payments. The leaks discussed above will be less
significant. The special problems of convertible
issues have been discussed, but such issues have
been rare so far. As with the U.S., the effect of
such borrowing has been to permit investment that
would otherwise be impossible and to limit the already intolerable pressure on the dollar premium.
Although this does not benefit the reserves directly, it does reduce the inducement to leaks, and it
also assists other investors who still have to use
the premium market. Private borrowing from local
banks and other institutions may have been relatively more important than public bond issues for
foreign-currency subsidiaries of United Kingdom
companies.

The development of the Euro-bond market has
added substantially to the earnings of the City of
London and has improved London's relative position
as a financial center, compared with New York.

EFFECT ON EXCHANGE RATES

What effect has the existence of the market
had on the dollar and sterling-exchange rates?
Einzig comments in a masterly understatement:
"Evidently the effects of European bond issues on
the dollar are extremely complex and conflicting."[6]
If the market benefits the U.S. balance of payments, there should be a corresponding strengthen-
ing of the U.S. dollar. A full answer to this
question would have to include an analysis of
short- and medium-term cash flows, sources, and use
of funds in the domestic U.S., Euro-dollar, and
European markets.

The mere fact that the dollar is the favorite
currency of issue must be beneficial. The interna-
tionalism of the dollar has increased the utility
of the currency from the point of view of both

borrowers and lenders. Foreigners are therefore
probably more inclined to hold dollars than they
were previously. If there really has been such a
shift of preferences, the position of the dollar
will have been correspondingly strengthened.

The very fact that more people may be induced
to hold dollars or dollar securities adds to the
potential threat to the dollar if there is ever a
serious possibility of devaluation. This is a
problem with any widely held currency, and the fact
that international investors are willing to hold
international dollar bonds in such quantities indicates that they do not take the threat of devaluation too seriously. The U.S. problem is still
far from the dimensions of that of the sterling
balances. The effect of the market must, in any
case, be small in relation to U.S. liquid liabilities and foreign central banks.

EFFECT ON INTEREST RATES

An obvious effect of the Euro-bond market has
been the narrowing of differentials between interest rates in different countries. This has been a
somewhat emotional subject, and European countries
have complained that their own interest-rate
structure has been affected. As explained in
Chapter 4, there are various ways to isolate domestic interest-rate structures, short of actual exchange control.

The interest-equalization tax has isolated
the U.S. fixed-interest market from that of the
rest of the world. If this tax and the voluntary
guidelines were abolished, the differential between Euro-bond rates and the rates of interest
obtainable on domestic U.S. issues of comparable
security and maturity would disappear. U.S. internal rates would tend to rise, while Euro-bond
rates would fall. We also have to consider the
effect on short-term rates that brings with it the
interactions between the Euro-bond and the

Euro-dollar markets discussed above. The existence
of a true international market must have reduced
discrepancies between interest rates in different
centers. This clearly does not benefit everybody,
as some borrowers in the past may have been borrowing on favorable terms because local investors
were not sufficiently aware of alternative opportunities.

The Euro-dollar market has certainly produced
a fairly effective international interest-rate
structure for prime lending at the lower end of
the market, but it is doubtful whether there is as
yet a really effective structure at the longer end
of the market, represented by Euro-bonds. A glance
at Table 12 shows the wide range of issues, natures
of guarantees, different currencies, currency options, and maturities. The secondary market (in
spite of protestations to the contrary by the banks
concerned) is still inadequate, and there are as
yet no large funds engaged in active switching.

Sterling is not a significant currency in the
Euro-bond market, and sales of sterling as investments in Euro-bonds are unlikely to have much effect. The integration of security sterling means
that such sales now have a direct impact on the
reserves. The previous minute discount on security
sterling makes this a technical rather than a
material factor, and the abolition of an additional
if theoretical risk to the foreign investor in
sterling securities is likely to bring in funds on
balance.

Sterling-area investors have long been
sophisticated buyers of dollar securities, and
they will certainly spot opportunities in the
Euro-bond market that are sufficiently attractive
to justify the premium. Euro-bond borrowings by
United Kingdom companies will tend to keep the
premium down. The present high level of premium
(a dual-exchange rate) must have implications for
confidence in the currency. However, sensible
United Kingdom investors will note that dollar

stocks bought with investment dollars are not a
hedge against devaluation. In 1949, the dollar
premium dropped from 36 per cent to 4 per cent on
the 30-1/2 per cent devaluation, leaving investors
in U.S. stocks with a small net loss on the deal.
Those looking for a devaluation hedge can usually
find much better ones. For instance, during 1966,
the price of London silver futures was a direct
reflection of prices in the New York market and
the spot and forward official rates of exchange.
As a result of the U.S. Treasury's policy at the
time, the dollar price of silver could hardly fall,
and there was a reasonable chance of a rise. For a
round-turn commission of 1/2 per cent and the loss
of interest representing the carrying charge on the
silver, the well-advised investor had a perfect and
legal devaluation hedge without any premium at all.
Silver has since become a fluctuating commodity,
like any other, and the four London banks specializing in the bullion market have been quoting an
exceptionally wide price, reflecting their un-
familiarity with proper commodity dealing. The
market is in the course of being transferred to the
London Metal Exchange. Meanwhile, hedgers may have
to look for alternative investments, but there is
unlikely to be a solution quite as neat as silver.

Devaluation of the pound came in November,
1967. In the event that dollar securities proved
a tolerably good hedge, the premium falling from
32 per cent to 26 per cent left half the devaluation gain with the investor. Silver was at a 6-pence
premium over New York parity just before devaluation. In theory, this meant that the market was
offering the sterling-area investor a 4 to 1 pay-
off on devaluation, compared with about 15 to 1
offered in the formal-exchange market to hard-
currency investors. The silver investor did in
fact do much better because of the subsequent attack on the dollar. The professionals were also
in copper futures, Australian securities, and
Bahamian dollar deposits.

More important than trying to discern influ-
ences on interest rates as such is the effect on
European capital markets. Are the issues diverting
funds from other European markets? The answer
would appear to be "no." Many investors need the
special tax and other features of the market and do
not regard domestic issues as an alternative.

Table 10 shows that, Euro-bonds apart, domestic interest rates in European countries have been
steadily rising. It is significant that the rise
in Euro-bond rates appears to have outstripped the
rise in most domestic European markets. Obviously,
the two interact with each other, but it is more
likely that general pressure on interest rates in
Europe has been responsible for high Euro-bond
yields than the other way around. The Federal
Reserve Board concludes that the additional factor
in the rise of rates on international bonds was due
to the surge in U.S. bond issues and to tightening
credit conditions in European markets. But as the
Board comments, recent interest-rate developments
in one country may well be explained by factors
more applicable to it alone.

To establish whether or not Euro-bond financing has caused high interest rates in Europe,
it is essential to consider the source of funds,
and whether these would otherwise have gone into
domestic financing in the countries concerned. The
answer is often no. Some of the money has come
from the sale of U.S. securities, and it is likely
that much of this money will only be invested in
issues with comparable prospectus requirements.
European markets and corporate legislation have
disclosure requirements that British and American
investors find inadequate, while investors in
other parts of the world like to feel that investment decisions can be made rationally after a
study of published documents. They suspect, perhaps with reason, that inside information and
hearsay are too important in Europe, and that they
will often not be dealing well for the profit of
the man on the spot.

TABLE 10

Long-Term European Government-Bond Yields, 1965-66

Date (on the last Friday)	Euro-Bond[a]	United Kingdom	Germany	The Netherlands	Switzerland
1965					
July	5.73	6.79	7.39	5.28	3.92
August	5.80	6.67	7.40	5.24	3.93
September	5.79	6.32	7.39	5.18	3.96
October	5.84	6.36	7.54	5.38	3.96
November	5.94	6.44	7.50	5.50	3.96
December	6.10	6.61	7.79	5.58	3.97
1966					
January	6.11	6.56	7.33	5.73	3.90
February	6.22	6.67	7.39	5.79	3.89
March	6.20	6.79	7.81	5.85	3.92
April	6.23	6.80	8.22	5.88	3.93
May	6.42	6.80	7.78	5.97	3.94
June	6.49	6.98	8.52	5.87	3.95
July	6.81	7.16	8.27	5.91	4.06
August	6.82	7.29	8.34	6.00	4.07
Difference	+ 1.09	0.50	0.95	0.72	0.15

[a]Represents an average of redemption yields for a representative sample.

Source: Bank of England, Quarterly Bulletin, various issues.

Considerable volumes of these issues are placed in Canada, with Middle Eastern oil kings, or with South American millionaires. The Swiss have been among the loudest complainers about diverting money from European markets, but is is significant that Swiss bonds have risen hardly at all recently. It certainly does not appear that Swiss money is being used. This is hardly surprising, given the regulations of the Swiss capital market. What may have offended the Swiss bankers is that investors who previously had funds deposited interest free in numbered accounts are now recognizing that a good return can be obtained while preserving secrecy, keeping away from suspect countries, and lacking involvement in taxation and estate duty.

As Genillard said:

> It is again very difficult for the same reason of professional discretion to let oneself be drawn into the argument regarding the extent to which funds have flown into the Euro-bond market which would otherwise have gone into local national markets. I can only assure you in this connection from my experience that the bulk of the funds represent bona fide long-term money from investors who dispose of reserves outside their countries of residence and wish to keep them in a different jurisdiction.[7]

It is hardly to be expected that Euro-bonds will cause much disruption to the vast domestic bond markets of such countries as Germany, for example. The magnitudes are totally different, and in many cases strict regulations apply. The German authorities even give preferential treatment to foreigners, despite complaints from the banks. Most European countries have regulations governing the investment of insurance and pension funds, although it is possible that these may be amended under pressure from the EEC Commission. Most Euro-bond

buyers do not consider domestic bonds as an alternative, and most Euro-bonds are financed from
sources hitherto untapped in Europe.

Has the Euro-bond market actually benefited
domestic European capital markets? It has been
suggested that the U.S., having put on pressure for
more efficient markets, is now destroying them
through the intemperate behavior of her companies.
The market has certainly shown signs of congestion
from time to time, and while local bond raising is
affected little, issues on a European scale un-
doubtedly are. The competition from U.S. subsidiaries, with their superior credit ratings, is perhaps too intense. The main benefit to domestic
markets from the growth of the Euro-bond market has
been to widen the base of investment thinking, to
create a wealth of financial expertise in Europe,
and to bring in money from outside Europe for such
important European ventures as Transalpine Finance.
Now that the mechanism for the utilization of liquid funds has been created, it will gather speed.

In Chapter 1, we noted the Strauss, Turnbull
figures that estimated interest payments on current loans will total $175 million per annum, while
sinking funds will reach this figure in 1970, and
at least $200 million by 1975. Very shortly, there-
fore, the market will be generating new financing
of $350 million per annum, and some of this cash
could well find its way into European markets.

Genillard noted:

> American borrowers have undoubtedly
> displaced some other potential is-
> suers, but their arrival has given
> the market a new dimension which
> will benefit other private borrowers.
> In any event the balance of non-U.S.
> borrowings is much larger than the
> total size of the market prior to the
> advent of borrowings by U.S. companies
> and most of the money has been destined

to finance investments in Europe anyway.[8]

THE GENERAL EFFECT ON CAPITAL MARKETS

Finally, how has the growth of the Euro-bond market affected the allocation of resources? To an economist, the purpose of a market, any market, is to allocate scarce resources between alternative uses, and its efficiency is measured by how it ensures that resources are channeled to their most effective and profitable use. The mere fact that the new market exists alongside the old indicates that it has added to the range of alternatives open to both borrowers and lenders. Therefore, there must have been some net gain in economic efficiency. The further fact that the market has proved so popular indicates that there were previous obstacles and inefficiencies which have now been removed. Some of these were especially created by governments; it is impossible to say from first principles whether there has been a net gain or loss in flexibility, but it seems likely that there has been a gain. Increasing perfection in markets does not benefit everyone; some borrowers will have to pay more because they will have lost a previously favored position, due to lack of knowledge of alternatives on the part of local investors. Similarly, some investors may have to forego above-average returns as nonresidents seek the opportunities offered.

Another benefit is the fact that there is little chance for the New York market to achieve a position of over-all dominance in international financial markets. It is undesirable that any one center should monopolize capital-issuing operations, partly because of the adverse effect on the balance of payments of the country concerned (and the risk of a sudden clamp-down of restrictions), and partly because the customer cannot be sure that he is getting a good deal. The U.S. authorities have actively encouraged the development of

European markets, and once a true international
market is created, spread between New York, London,
Amsterdam, Paris, Zurich (and eventually perhaps
centers in Asia, Africa, and Latin America), it may
be possible to relax U.S. restrictions and give the
investing and borrowing public a wider choice of
financial techniques, flexibility, freedom from
restrictions, and international competition in
underwriting, terms, and services.

The growth of the Euro-bond market may have
contributed to an increase in the circulation
velocity of the U.S. dollar. This, in turn, may
have relieved some of the pressures on international liquidity. On the other hand, the greater
practical freedom of capital movement and the increased volume of funds looking for the best return, regardless of national frontiers, could have
an unsettling effect on world equilibrium. An integrated capital market makes it more difficult
for countries to pursue their own domestic monetary
policies, without the type of exchange controls
that we deplore. These questions go beyond the
scope of our work, touching as they do on the most
controversial and interesting aspects of general
international monetary theory. Little light can be
thrown on them here, and the questions must either
be dismissed in a sentence or expanded in a book on
international economic theory.

NOTES TO CHAPTER 6

1. Economist (July 8, 1967), p. 126.

2. For futher details, see Herbert Christie, "How Eurodollars Affect U.S. Payments," The Banker (London) (January, 1967), p. 36.

3. Paul Einzig, The Eurodollar System (London: MacMillan & Company, 1964), p. 10; also see G. L. Bell, "Credit Creation Through Euro Dollars?," The Banker (London) (August, 1964).

4. Einzig, op. cit.; also see Paul Einzig, A Dynamic Theory of Forward Exchange (London: MacMillan & Company, 1961).

5. Bank for International Settlements, Annual Report (Basle, Switzerland, 1966), p. 51.

6. Paul Einzig, Foreign Dollar Loans in Europe (London: MacMillan & Company, 1965), p. 89.

7. European Economic Community, The Development of a European Capital Market, Commission Report (November, 1966), p. 35.

8. Ibid., p. 43.

CHAPTER 7 RECENT DEVELOPMENTS AND THE FUTURE OF THE MARKET

INTRODUCTION

Numerous political factors affecting the international capital market have deteriorated recently. The pound sterling was devalued on November 19, 1967, from $2.80 to $2.40, but opportunity was not taken to abolish exchange control on capital transactions. Such control ought to be irrelevant if the exchange rate were now right. The dollar premium has even risen. Immediately before devaluation, the premium was 33 per cent, an effective rate of exchange of £1 = $2.08. On devaluation, it fell to 26 per cent and subsequently rose to a new high of 35 per cent, an exchange rate of $1.78. The present level of popular economic discussion in the United Kingdom (exemplified by the "back Britain" movement) is not only pre-Keynes but pre-Adam Smith. The forward market, now unsupported by the Bank of England, is very weak. Devaluation has affected world interest rates but has not otherwise affected the situation described in earlier chapters, particularly Chapter 4.

In the United States, the situation is in some respects worse. The "voluntary" guidelines has now become mandatory and has been considerably tightened up. Fortunately, the Ways and Means Committee appears likely to block the ill-conceived notion of following Britain's dreadful example to restrict freedom to travel abroad.

Repercussions have been felt in Canada and Australia, but fortunately, and for reasons explained below, Europe is standing firm as a free international market for capital.

The European dollar-bond market itself continues to prosper because of restrictions and in spite of high interest rates. New issues in 1967 totaled $1,884 million, compared with $1,101 million for 1966. Non-U.S. borrowers accounted for most of the increase. Financing subsidiaries of U.S. parents took $527 million (28 per cent of the whole) in 1967 and $479 million (43 per cent) in 1966.

During the first two months of 1968, new issues totaled $576.9 million, nearly double the amount for the corresponding period in the previous year. In striking contrast to the 1967 trend, 81 per cent ($466.5 million) represented U.S. corporate financing, a direct reflection of the new measures. Substantially, the whole of the U.S. issues were of convertible bonds: In present market conditions, companies are reluctant to make issues with the 7 per cent minimum coupon now required for a straight issue.

THE NEW U.S. REGULATIONS

Perhaps the most significant development of all is the U.S. Executive Order 11387 and subsequent regulations. These should be studied against the previous restrictions on the outflow of direct investment discussed earlier. The new regulations, effective January 1, 1968, established an Office of Foreign Direct Investments (OFDI) as an organ of the Department of Commerce. Unlike the voluntary guidelines programs, willful violations of the more recent provisions carry maximum penalties on conviction of $10,000 fines, imprisonment for ten years, or both.

The regulations divide the countries of the world into three categories:

Category A includes less-developed countries defined under the same terms as those for the interest-equalization tax.

Category B includes those developed countries in which a high level of capital inflow is deemed essential for the maintenance of economic growth and financial stability and where these rates cannot be met adequately from non-U.S. sources: The United Kingdom, The Republic of Ireland, Canada, Japan, Australia, New Zealand, Hong Kong, Bermuda, the Bahamas, Abu Dhabi, Bahrain, Iran, Iraq, Kuwait, Libya, Qatar, and Saudi Arabia.

Category C includes all other developed countries: the six EEC countries, Switzerland, Norway, Sweden, Denmark, Austria, Spain, Portugal, Liechtenstein, Monaco, San Marino, and South Africa. For different reasons, all countries in the Soviet and Chinese sphere of influence are included in Category C as well.

"Direct investment" is defined as investment by any "United States person" (a term that includes individuals, corporations, and all other forms of organization) in any "foreign national" (again an all-inclusive term) in which the "United States person" directly or indirectly owns or acquires an interest of 10 per cent or more of the total voting power or claims such assets on dissolution. Subject to the ingenuity of lawyers, it seems that any investment not subject to control as a direct investment is liable to interest-equalization tax as a portfolio investment. Puerto Rico is regarded for this purpose as inside the United States, but a U.S. corporation deriving 80 per cent or more of its income from non-U.S. sources is regarded as a foreign national.

Following the example of the United Kingdom Exchange Control Act, all direct or indirect

transfers of capital by way of foreign direct investment are prohibited unless specifically authorized. The prohibition extends to transfers of
credit and a wide range of indirect transactions;
the control extends to reinvested earnings (defined as earnings available at any time for distribution and not so distributed). In computing
the earnings of affiliated companies, adjustments
in accordance with Section 482 of the Internal
Revenue Code may be made. This precludes indirect
financing by means of adjustments to invoice
prices on transactions within the group.

General consent is given for direct investments (including the share in retained earnings) by
up to $100,000 per investor. This provision has a
great advantage over the United Kingdom practice
and allows the foreign investment newcomer some
flexibility that partly neutralizes the advantages
which established international companies would
otherwise have.

In addition, each investor may invest (again
including retained earnings) 110 per cent of its
average direct investments in a Category A country
based on 1965 and 1966 figures and 65 per cent of
its average invested in a Category B country. For
a Category C country, no transfers of capital are
permitted without specific consent, but reinvested
earnings may be retained up to the amount of 35 per
cent. Unused entitlements with respect to one
category may only be transferred into a higher
category (for example, C to B), but not to a lower
category.

Net borrowings from nonaffiliated foreign nationals are disregarded in computing direct investment. As before, therefore, the intention is
not to restrict expansion of U.S.-owned corporations, provided expansion can be financed, for
instance, by Euro-dollar borrowings either in the
form of bond issues or bank loans.

There is an additional rule that each direct investor is required to transfer not less than once each year the same proportion of his current earnings as was distributed on an average based on the 1964-66 period.

The secretary of commerce has the right at any time to withdraw these general consents from any specific direct investor and may, through the OFDI, authorize specific transactions or exempt specific individuals from the provisions.

THE MARKET ITSELF

The market itself continues to thrive in spite of high interest rates, and its international nature continues to be a striking feature. The largest industrial issue to date, Chrysler, was headed by a London merchant bank (S. G. Warburg), even though British investors were virtually precluded from subscribing, while the Chevron issue was headed by a Dutch bank (AMRO). The Continental Telephone issue may be the first example of an issue made on the European market by a subsidiary of a U.S. company to finance operations outside Europe, although all of the Japanese issues have been of this nature. Iceland has also joined the long list of countries represented.

Roussel-UCLAF was the first Euro-franc issue. The Royal Dutch-Shell group made an issue via a Netherlands Antilles subsidiary, Shell International Finance N.V.. International Utilities Overseas Capital Corporation was the first U.S. issue of guaranteed bonds with stock purchase warrants attached. New five- to ten-year bonds have been issued, closing the maturity gap between the Eurobond and Euro-dollar markets. In the Euro-dollar market proper, negotiable bank certificates of deposit are becoming a popular instrument. The Japanese have abolished their 10 per cent withholding tax, which will help their companies to come back to the market on competitive terms.

The quality of the after-market, though still imperfect, is starting to improve. There is still some confusion about delivery procedure, reflecting the different habits of the many national financial markets involved. Some houses will deliver stock only against payment, while others make (and expect) payment on the date specified in the contract, regardless of delivery. For some time, there have been suggestions that the Bank for International Settlements might act as an unofficial clearing house. In any event, Morgan Guaranty Trust Company of New York has set up a clearance service in Brussels for U.S. dollar Euro-bonds. The objectives are stated to be:

1.   To expedite U.S. dollar Euro-bond settlements and/or deliveries;

2.   To reduce physical movement of bonds to a minimum and eliminate, as far as possible, expenses and delays resulting from shipments;

3.   To make possible the delivery of bonds against corresponding payments and vice versa.

Participants deposit their bonds with Morgan Guaranty in Brussels or with correspondents in Amsterdam, Basle, Frankfurt, Geneva, London, Luxembourg, Milan, New York, Paris, or Zurich. Eventually it is hoped that most transactions will be settled by transfers on stock accounts in the system rather than by physical delivery.

Earlier we discussed whether the issue of convertible Euro-bonds guaranteed by U.S. parents might result in a net outflow from the U.S. as nonresidents switched into the convertible from the equity. The behavior of certain stock prices in early 1968 strongly suggested that this was happening.

There seems little doubt that the Euro-bond market will continue to prosper as a true international market. All the worries induced by

interest-rate changes have proved false, principally because an interest rate in a free market is a
price that balances supply and demand. Fears of
congestion are proving unjustified, and the figures indicate clearly that the market itself will
soon be generating a cash flow sufficient to ensure
its continued health.

Inevitably there are proposals to regulate the
market, sometimes on the grounds that U.S. borrowers have swamped the market at the expense of
others. Sir Siegmund Warburg has suggested that a
small committee of European bankers should be
formed to regulate issues and organize a queue,
following the pattern of the Swiss issuing syndicate. The Bank for International Settlements has
also been cast for this role.

Others believe that since a free and open
capital market has now developed, it should be encouraged rather than restrained. However unpopular
changes in the rate of interest may be with governments, the history of the market has shown that a
flexible price for capital is an effective way to
ensure a properly functioning and uncongested
market.

More important than proposals for restricting
access to the market on financial grounds is the
possibility of further government regulation. The
British and U.S. governments have increasingly imposed restrictions on the financial transactions
of their own citizens, but many other countries
still take a more liberal attitude. Even Canada,
with her own problems, has not imposed any
exchange-control restrictions to date. Nonresident
holders of dollars or external sterling have a substantial degree of monetary freedom, and residents
of some of the Caribbean islands, certain Latin
American countries, and the oil sheikdoms can still
do what they like with their own property. The
European Economic Community is a particularly interesting situation. Some of its members are
liberal by tradition, and others (such as France)

are restrictionist. The Treaty of Rome will eventually prohibit all restrictions on capital movements between members (as discussed earlier), and
the general spirit of the Treaty favors free transactions with the rest of the world. Given internal
freedom, any individual country that imposes restrictions on external capital movements will simply be offering its neighbors a profitable entrepôt
business. The EEC could become restrictionist
only by common political consent, which under the
present circumstances is unlikely, and for some
years at least, therefore, we can rule out global
enforcement of restrictions on financial freedom.

The success of the free international market
may render national restrictions so ineffective
that they are abandoned. If and when Britain
secures entry to the EEC, she might be forced to
abandon her present exchange restrictions. This of
itself would de-escalate the present beggar-my-
neighbor situation--and U.S. controls might be re-
laxed. The London and New York markets would expand their more traditional methods of financing,
but the Euro-bond market would continue as the
nucleus of a true international market in which no
center dominated.

THE EURO-WORLD

The Euro-dollar market is the shorter end and
the Euro-bond market the longer end of a true international money and capital market. There are
no longer any major gaps in the maturity structure,
and the market includes (indeed has recently been
dominated by) convertible bonds. There are also a
few detachable stock-purchase warrants, and we
confidently expect the number of these to increase.
Will the Euro-world expand to include a significant
number of true Euro-equities?

Claudio Segré has suggested that American
companies with European subsidiaries should not
confine themselves to issuing bonds (even

convertible bonds) but should form European holding companies in which local investors could be
offered equity participation. One objection to
this proposal (as explained in Chapter 5) is that
it is still impossible to create a tax-neutral
holding company for equity participations. If investors in France, Germany, and Belgium hold
shares in a company, wherever incorporated, that
derives business income in France, Germany, and
Belgium, the total tax burden will be higher than
if the same investment were made through three
natural companies held directly. Segré recognizes
this point and is himself one of the most active
propagandists for the type of tax harmonization
that would remove this objection.

There is a considerable amount of work in
progress toward a Community-wide company law.[1]
Company law is never in practice an obstacle to
closer integration, but a unified corporation code
would isolate and focus attention on the more
serious tax and other obstacles and stimulate action to remove them.[2]

Another objection to the Segré proposals is
that the existence of minority stockholders in one
area of operation can lead to a conflict of interest. A parent company wishes to be able to make
its decisions as to where to manufacture and where
to take its profits in the interests of the general
body of its own stockholders, without reference to
third parties. The experience of minority shareholders in European and Canadian companies when
there is a U.S. parent has frequently been unsatisfactory, and the trend, until recently, was
to buy out any outstanding minorities.

Segré may indeed have had in mind deliberately
creating a conflict situation. One of the fears of
countries where there is a substantial American investment is that the parent company may wish to remove production from the country and concentrate it
elsewhere. The existence of a local minority might
inhibit such a move and ensure that the board of

the local company think in terms of their own company (and country) rather than in the interests of
the group.

Those European investors who think in equity
terms might, in any case, prefer to buy the shares
of the American parent company. There is every-
thing to be said for facilitating such purchases
and for ensuring that the ordinary French and German investor can be made aware of the opportunities.
The British investor has never needed such encouragement, has beaten his own successful path to Wall
Street, and remains undeterred by an apparently
prohibitive dollar premium. For historical reasons,
nationals of other countries have taken a narrower
view of investment possibilities, and it may be
that a formal listing on the European exchanges
may be necessary to stimulate interest.

THE INTERNATIONAL COMPANY

A fascinating recent book, Le Defi Americain,
by Jean-Jacques Servan-Schreiber, suggests that
"American business in Europe" is rapidly becoming
one of the great world powers.[3] There is a tendency, in countries such as France, to assume that
the American businessman abroad is probably an
agent of the State Department or the CIA. This is
the opposite of the truth. Internationally ori-
ented American business is, as often as not, trying to keep out of the clutches of politicians
where possible, or at least to play off one group
of national politicians against another. Servan-
Schreiber does not exactly ignore, but he does
underestimate, the growing role of the true international company. Such a company may formally be
American, British, Swiss, Dutch, Swedish, or
Japanese, but it is beginning to conceive of itself
as a global organization. Its operations will be
international, but so will be its stockholders,
its staff, and its sources of ideas. In the rapidly approaching ideal, no national preference will
be shown in the choice of its directors and

officers.   Judd Polk suggests an approach which
better describes the real international business
world today.[4]

Britain and the United States have given birth
to many international businesses.   The U.S. Revenue
Act of 1962, recent highly adverse tax changes in
the United Kingdom, and restrictions on overseas
investment in both countries have made them both
uncomfortable bases for modern international business.   Business International points out:

> A golden opportunity for European,
> Canadian, and Japanese corporations,
> indeed for all non-U.S. and non-U.K.
> corporations, has been provided by the
> response of many U.S. and U.K. corpora-
> tions to the controls their governments
> have put on the export of corporate
> capital.   The opportunity is the first
> of its kind and may never come again.
> For never before have both governments
> so severely restrained their business
> leaders from investing as much as they
> wished, at any time and in any place in
> the world.
> It is an opportunity for non-U.S.
> and non-U.K. corporations to push
> capital-short U.S. and U.K. foreign
> subsidiaries to the wall with increased
> expenditures for promotion and adver-
> tising, price cutting, and on-the-spot
> research and development.
> It is also an opportunity for
> non-U.S. and non-U.K. corporations to
> acquire new foreign enterprises while
> their U.S. and U.K. competitors sit on
> the sidelines.
> Who stands to gain?   No major
> industrialized country, other than the
> U.S. and the U.K., now seriously im-
> pedes the worldwide expansion of cor-
> porations domiciled within their
> borders.   Germany, Switzerland, Canada,

and France all have fully free currencies with which their companies can
invest anywhere they see solid projects.
Countries such as Sweden, the Low Countries, Italy, and Japan do have a variety of case-by-case approval requirements for corporate capital outflows,
but they are operated in a manner as-
suring that approvals are almost always
given whenever the capital outflows will
benefit the country. Since all profitable foreign investments greatly strength-
en the medium and long-term balance-of-
payments position of the capital export-
ing country, few non-U.S. and non-U.K.
international firms face such difficulties from their own governments. . . .
There will surely be opportunities for
European and Japanese companies to acquire the existing operations of U.S.
and U.K. subsidiaries in Europe. . . .
    The controls have put a new premium
on international business know-how. It
is no longer adequate for a U.S. or
British executive only to know how to
make and market a product. If his company is to be among the few hundred that
in 20 years or so will account for more
than 50% of the world's GNP (a development many scholars say is inevitable),
then he must develop an expertise in
international business and finance to
match his present technological, market,
and management capabilities. . . . As
in the great Depression, today's conditions will separate the men from the
boys.[5]

This is splendid stuff. But apart from the
possible expansion of non-U.S. and non-U.K. international companies, we can expect two other developments. One is the growth of international companies initially based outside the major, high tax,
restrictive countries, and the other is the spin-off

of operations by operators of existing companies,
based on British or American management or know-how.

The funds for the Euro-bond market come in
part from those who have removed themselves from,
or kept themselves outside of, the jurisdiction of
those countries whose politicians buy votes by imposing envy taxes or who mask their incompetence
at currency management by attempting to restrict
access to the free-exchange markets. A new genera-
tion of entrepreneurs is growing up who base their
operations right from the start outside these
countries. Modern levels of taxation make it desirable, and modern telecommunications and air
travel make it possible, to administer an international enterprise from wherever happens for the
moment to be fiscally convenient. Some of these
people will wish to capitalize their enterprise by
a public issue, and they may well start to feed a
Euro-equity market.

The classic example is Syntex, a Panamanian
company with headquarters in Mexico City and a
listing on the American Stock Exchange. It has
subsidiaries and licenses throughout the world
and tends to finance its research out of profits
generated in high-tax countries such as the U.S.
Profits from other countries can often be enjoyed
virtually tax free. There is no withholding tax
on dividends. The U.S. resident-shareholder is
taxed on dividends, but these will have borne a
lower rate of underlying tax than dividends from a
corresponding U.S. corporation. It may be that
U.S. securities regulations will make it increasingly difficult for such corporations to be listed
in that country. If this happens, it will give
further stimulus to the international market.

Syntex is by no means unique. Schlumberger is
a Curaçao corporation controlled by a Frenchman who
lives in New York, and the stock is listed on the
New York Stock Exchange. For historical reasons,
London can boast an even wider range of such securities, including Hong Kong trading companies with

international ramifications (such as Wheelock
Marden and Hutchinson International), Anglo Norness
Shipping of Bermuda, and Tanganyika Concessions
operating in Africa but resident in the Bahamas.
There is also that collector's piece, Anglo French
Ticapampa Silver Mining Corporation Ltd., a United
Kingdom registered company with administrative of-
fices in New York and business in Peru. The capi-
tal is expressed in pounds sterling, accounts are
kept in Peruvian sols, and dividends are declared
in U.S. dollars. The shares are quoted only in
Paris.

It may often be advantageous for existing
companies to set up parallel companies or quoted
affiliates that can issue further shares against
local acquisitions and that may eventually cease to
be formally controlled by the original parent.
There are already several examples. Oldest in
history are probably the two Anglo-Dutch twins,
Shell-Royal Dutch and Unilever Ltd.-Unilever N.V.,
both set up before tax- and exchange-control factors became paramount. There is also the Nestlé-
Unilac formula that is bound shortly to have imita-
tors. Nestlé is a Swiss company with interests
and shareholders throughout the world. Nonresident
shareholders without the protection of a double-tax
agreement suffer 30 per cent withholding tax on
dividends. This is bypassed, for earnings arising
outside Switzerland, by forming a parallel company,
Unilac, in Panama, to own certain non-Swiss affiliates. Stock certificates for Nestlé and Unilac are
printed on the same piece of paper and trade as a
unit.

Two of the more interesting recent examples
of hiving are not European but United Kingdom com-
panies seeking to expand in the United States.
Electrical and Musical Industries (EMI) had a sub-
stantial and wholly owned U.S. subsidiary, Capitol
Records, Incorporated, acquired in happier times.
Capitol has now been merged into Audio Devices
Incorporated, a company listed on the American
Stock Exchange, by an exchange of stock on terms

that give EMI control of the merged companies and
hence a listed base for expansion. Rio Tinto Zinc
(RTZ), that most enterprising of international
mining groups, has just merged with Borax Limited,
a United Kingdom company whose major asset is a
controlling interest in Borax Incorporated of the
U.S. (Business International suggests that present
U.S. restrictions inhibited a U.S. counterbid.)
Less sophisticated United Kingdom papers said that
the next step might be a bid for the U.S. minority
in Borax Incorporated. This is to underestimate
RTZ, which will certainly use the U.S. corporation
as a base for further expansion.

We expect a growing number of companies based
on tax havens, operating on the basis of fiscal
expediency and flexibility, and tailoring their
securities to the need of the international markets.
The old battle between the politicians and bureau-
crats who wish to regulate, restrict, and "tidy up"
and the businessmen who need flexibility to re-
spond to new challenges and opportunities is reach-
ing a new and fascinating phase. The Euro-world
is here to stay, and if Europe itself becomes in-
hospitable, the only true international capital
market will quickly but quietly move itself to some
safer haven.

NOTES TO CHAPTER 7

1. See Pieter Sanders, Project d'un Statut
d'une Société Anonyme Europeenne (Brussels:
European Economic Community, December, 1966).

2. An interesting analysis of the situation
is given in Les Fusions Internationales des
Sociétés dans la Communauté Économique Europeenne
(Brussels: UNICE, 1966).

3. Jean-Jacques Servan-Schreiber, Le Défi
Américain (Paris: Denoël, 1967).

4.   Judd Polk, "The New World Economy,"
Columbia Journal of World Business (January-
February, 1968).

5.   "U.S., U.K., Capital Controls Provide
Opportunity for Growth of True International Firms,"
Business International (February 16, 1968), p. 49.
We thank Business International for permission to
quote.

STATISTICAL APPENDIX

TABLE 11

Foreign-Bond Resume

	Amount (in millions of dollars)	
	1964	1965
Total of foreign-bond issues	978.6	1,201
Subject to IET	773.1	972
Not subject to IET	205.5	229
Internationally syndicated	695.3	864
Not internationally syndicated	283.3	337
By currencies $	583	708
DM	224	315
£/DM	14	64
Fl	15	30
EUA	10	--
FF	31	24
SF	98	57
£	4	--
BF	--	3
Total	979	1,201
By centers New York	242	483
London	336	219
Germany	223	315
Switzerland	98	57
Other	80	127
	979	1,201

Source: Figures supplied by White, Weld & Company.

List of Underwriters for Bristol-Myers Loan

United States
Lehman Brothers   1 William Street, New
                               York, N.Y. 10004
Hill Samuel & Co. Ltd.   100 Wood Street, London,
                               E.C. 2.

TABLE 11 (Cont'd)

White, Weld & Co.	20 Broad Street, New York, N.Y. 10005
Blyth & Co. Inc.	14 Wall Street, New York, N.Y. 10005
Eastman Dillon, Union Securities & Co.	1 Chase Manhattan Plaza, New York, N.Y. 10005
Goldman, Sachs & Co.	20 Broad Street, New York, N.Y. 10005
Lazard Freres & Co.	44 Wall Street, New York, N.Y. 10005
Carl M. Loeb, Rhoades & Co.	42 Wall Street, New York, N.Y. 10005
Merrill Lynch, Pierce, Fenner & Smith Securities Underwriter Limited	70 Pine Street, New York, N.Y. 10005
Morgan Stanley & Co.	2 Wall Street, New York, N.Y. 10005
Paine, Webber, Jackson & Curtis	25 Broad Street, New York, N.Y. 10004
Smith, Barney & Co. Incorporated	20 Broad Street, New York, N.Y. 10005
Wertheim & Co.	1 Chase Manhattan Plaza, New York, N.Y. 10005

Belgium

Banque Lambert	24 Avenue Marnix, Brussels
Societe Generale de Banque, S.A.	3 Montagne du Parc, Brussels
Kredietbank N.V.	7 Aranbergstraat, Brussels

Denmark

Kjobenhavns Handelsbank	Holmens Kanal 2, Copenhagen K

France

Banque de Paris et des Pays-Bas	3 Rue d'Antin, Paris 2
Credit Commercial de France, S.A.	103 Avenue des Champs-Elysees, Paris 8
Credit Lyonnais	19 Boulevard des Italiens, Paris

Morgan & Cie S.A.	4 Place de la Concorde, Paris 1
de Neuflize, Schlumberger & Cie	12 Place de la Bourse, Paris 2
L'Union des Mines-La Henin S.A.	9 Rue Louis Murat, Paris 8

Germany

Berliner Handels-Gesellschaft	Bockenheimer Landstr. 10 Frankfurt/Main
Deutsche Bank Aktien-gesellschaft	Junghofstrasse 5-11, Frankfurt/Main
Dresdner Bank Aktien-gesellschaft	7 Gallusanlage, Frankfurt/Main

Italy

Banca Commerciale Italiana	6 Piazza della Scala, Milan
Credito Italiano	Piazza Cordusio, Milan

The Netherlands

Algemene Bank Nederland N.V.	138-150 Spuistraat/ 32 Vijzelstraat, Amsterdam
Amsterdam-Rotterdam Bank N.V.	595 Herengracht, Amsterdam
Hope & Co.	577-581 Keizersgracht, Amsterdam C.
Pierson, Heldring & Pierson	206-214 Herengracht, Amsterdam

Sweden

Stockholms Enskilda Bank	8 Kungstradgardsgatan, Stockholm
Svenska Handelsbanken	11 Arsenalsgatan, Stockholm 16

United Kingdom

Samuel Montagu & Co. Ltd.	114 Old Broad Street, London, E.C. 2.
N. M. Rothschild & Sons	New Court, St. Swithin's Lane, London, E.C. 4.
J. Henry Schroder Wagg & Co. Ltd.	120 Cheapside, London, E.C. 2
S. G. Warburg & Co. Ltd.	30 Gresham Street, London, E.C. 2

Source: Bristol-Myers International Finance Company Prospectus on 4 1/2 Guaranteed Debentures Due 1980 (December 13,1965), pp. 16-17.

TABLE 12

All International Bonds Issued, 1965-66

Date of Issue	Amount of Loan and Currency of Issue (in millions)	Name of Issue	Type of Issue[a]	Form of Issue[a]	Maturity Date	Coupon of the Loan (Nominal Interest Rate)	Issue Price	Nationality of Issuing Party
1965								
January	$25	Sir-Kvina Kraftselskap	*	D	1985	5-3/4	97-3/4	Norway
--	$20	Republic of Portugal[b]		D	1985	5-3/4	97-1/2	Portugal
--	$15	Republic of the Philippines[b]		D	1980	6-1/2	98-1/2	Philippines
--	$20	International Bank for R & D	I	D	1990	4-1/2	100-3/8	--
--	£4	Enso-Gutzeit Oy	*	OD	1980	6-1/2	97-3/4	Finland
February	$20	Cassa per il Mezzogiorno	G*	D	1985	6	97-1/2	Italy
--	DM 100	City of Osaka	G	D	1980	6-1/4	99	Japan
--	DM 50	Municipality of Oslo		D	1980	5-3/4	100	Norway
March	$30	Kingdom of Norway	*	D	1985	5-1/2	98	Norway
--	$13	Hollis Financial & Commercial Corporation	*	D	1977	6	100	The Netherlands
--	$10	City of Helsinki[b]		D	1977	6-1/4	97-1/4	Finland
--	DM 250	IBRD	I	D	1985	5-1/2	100	--
--	DM 150	European Coal & Steel Community	I	D	1983	5-1/2	99	--
--	SF 35	Rheinkraftwerk Sackingen AG		D	1980	4-3/4	101	Germany
--	SF 4.5	A/s Vaksdal Molle Bergen		D	1973	5	100	Norway
--	SF 40	Eurofima	I	D	1982	5		--
--	$25 Cdn	IBRD	I	D	1989	5-1/4	99-1/2	--
April	$25	State of Malaysia[b]		D	1970	5-1/2	99.54	Malaysia
--	$15	Republic of Venezuela[b]		D	1980	6-1/4	99	Venezuela

Month	Amount	Issuer		Type	Year	Rate	Price	Country
--	$22.5	Nippon Telegraph & Telephone[b]		D	1980	5-3/4	97-1/4	Japan
--	SF 60	IBRD	I	D	1983	4-3/4	100	--
--	Fl 40	European Investment Bank	I	D	1990	5-3/4	100	--
--	Fl 40	ECSC	I	D	1985	5-3/4	100	--
May	$7.5[c]	Fonds de Reetablissement de conseil de l'Europe	I*	PD	1980	5-3/4	99-1/4	--
--	$25	Commonwealth of Australia	*	D	1985	5-1/2	98-1/2	Australia
--	DM 100	British Petroleum Co. Ltd.		D	1980	5-1/2	97	United Kingdom
--	SF 100	Serck Ltd., Birmingham		D	1980	5	100	United Kingdom
--	£4	Lamco Syndicate	*	OD	1980	5-3/4	96-1/4	Sweden
June	$15	City of Oslo		D	1985	5-3/4	98-3/4	Norway
--	$15	Allmanna Svenska Elekriska	*	D	1980	6	97	Sweden
--	$12	Oesterreichisch-Alpine-Montangesellschaft	G*	D	1985	5-3/4	97	Austria
--	$20	Kingdom of Denmark		D	1985	6	99	Denmark
--	$20	Metropolis of Tokyo[b]		D	1980	6	95-1/4	Japan
--	$50	Quebec Hydro-Electric Commission[b]		D	1985	4-5/8	98.397	Canada
--	SF 50	Mont-Blanc Tunnel		D	1980	4-3/4	100	France
--	£10	Mobil Oil Holdings	*	OD	1980	5-3/4	97	United States
--	£3.15	Government of Jamaica		D	1978	7	97	Jamaica
July	$20	Government of New Zealand	*	D	1985	5-3/4	97-1/2	New Zealand
--	DM 100	ENEL	G	PD	1980	6	95	Italy
--	SF 40	Tauernkraftwerke	G	D	1980	5	100	Austria
--	Fl 25	ENEL	G	PD	1980	6	95	Italy
--	FF 125	ENEL	G	PD	1980	6	95-3/4	Italy
--	£5	U.S. Rubber Uniroyal Holding	*	OD	1980	6	97	United States
--	Flux 30	ENEL	G	D	1980	6	95	Italy

TABLE 12 (Cont'd)

Date of Issue	Amount of Loan and Currency of Issue (in millions)	Name of Issue	Type of Issue^a	Form of Issue^a	Maturity Date	Coupon of the Loan (Nominal Interest Rate)	Issue Price	Nationality of Issuing Party
August	£10	Government of New Zealand		D	1971	6-3/4	98-1/2	New Zealand
September	$15	Kockums Mekaniska Verkstads	G*	D	1980	6	99-1/4	Sweden
--	$10	Ciments Lafarge	*	D	1980	6	97-1/2	France
--	$20	Cyanamid Int.	*	D	1980	5-3/4	98-1/4	United States
--	$20	European Investment Bank	I*	D	1985	6	99-1/2	--
--	$50	Province of Ontario^b	*	D	1990	4-3/4	98.56	Canada
October	$25	Amoco Oil Holdings	*	D	1985	5-3/4	99-1/2	United States
--	$20	Comp. Franc de Petroles	*	D	1985	6	98-1/4	France
--	$15	Eriksbergs Mekaniska Verkstads	G*	D	1980	6	99-1/4	Sweden
--	$15	Roldal-Suldal Kraft A/S	*	D	1985	6-1/4	98-1/2	Norway
--	$15	Republic of Finland^b		D	1980	6-1/2	99	Finland
--	DM 100	Transocean Gulf Oil	*	D	1980	5-3/4	98-1/2	United States
--	DM 50	Electricity Supply Commn Johannesburg	G*	D	1980	6-1/2	96-1/2	South Africa
--	DM 80	Basf Holding Luxembourg		D	1980	6	99-1/2	Germany
--	SF 45	Mobil Oil Holdings		D	1980	4-3/4	100	United States
--	BF 500	European Investment Bank	I	D	1977	6-1/2	99	--
--	Lire 15,000	European Investment Bank	I	D	1985	6	96	--
November	$25	Monsanto International Finance	*	CD	1965	4-1/2	100	United States
--	$25	Commonwealth of Australia	*	D	1985	5-3/4	99-3/4	Australia
--	$15	Hollis Financial & Commercial Corporation	*	D	1978	6	100	The Netherlands

182

	Amount	Issuer		Type	Year	Rate	Price	Country
--	$20	W. R. Grace Overseas	*	D	1980	5-3/4	97-3/4	United States
--	$15	Aktiebolaget Gotaverken	G*	D	1980	6	99	Sweden
--	$15	City of Copenhagen	*	D	1985	6	99-1/2	Denmark
--	$27.5	Mexico State[b]	G	D	1980	6-1/2	98-3/4	Mexico
--	$20	Japan Development Bank[b]	G	D	1980	6-1/2	98-3/4	Japan
--	DM 100	Du Pont Europa	*	D	1980	6	100	United States
--	DM 60	Eurofima	I	D	1980	6	99	
--	SF 45	British Petroleum Company		D	1980	4-3/4		United Kingdom
--	SF 4.5	Societe Glittre		D	1975	5	99-1/2	Norway
--	SF 45	Bowater Paper		D	1981	5	99	United Kingdom
December								
--	$8	Kraftlaget Opplandskaft	*	D	1985	6-1/4	97-1/2	Norway
--	$15	British Myers International	*	CD	1980	4-1/2	100	United States
--	$20	Federated Dept Stores	*	CD	1985	4-1/2	100	United States
--	$50	General Electric Overseas	*	CD	1985	4-1/4	100	United States
--	DM 120	IBM World Trade	*	D	1981	6	100	United States
--	Fl.100	Unilever	*	D	1992	6	98	The Netherlands
1966								
January								
--	$12	Mortgage Bank of Denmark	*	D	1986	6-1/4	96-1/2	Denmark
--	$20	SGI International Holdings	*	WD	1980	6-1/2	99-1/2	Italy
--	$25	Phillips Petroleum International	*	D	1981	6	98	United States
--	$7.5	Government of Jamaica[b]		D	1981	6-3/4	96.80	Jamaica
--	UAC 20	ECSC	I*	D	1986	5-3/4	99-3/8	--
--	DM 60	AEG Finance Holding		D	1981	6	98-1/2	Germany
--	SF 45	Transocean Gulf Oil		D	1981	5	100	United States
--	Lira 15,000	ECSC	I	D	1986	6	96-1/2	--
February								
--	$20	ENI	*	D	1981	6	95-3/4	Italy
--	$15	Honeywell International	*	D	1981	6	96	United States
--	$15	International Standard Electric	*	D	1986	6	97-1/2	United States
--	$15	ISE Finance	*	CD	1986	4-1/2	97-1/2	United States

TABLE 12 (Cont'd)

Date of Issue	Amount of Loan and Currency of Issue (in millions)	Name of Issue	Type of Issue[a]	Form of Issue[a]	Maturity Date	Coupon of the Loan (Nominal Interest Rate)	Issue Price	Nationality of Issuing Party
February	$30	Pepsico Overseas	*	CD	1981	4-1/2	100	United States
--	$15	Warner Lambert International	*	CD	1981	4-1/4	100	United States
--	$25	Marathon International	*	CD	1986	4-1/2	100	United States
--	$15	Avon Overseas	*	D	1981	6-1/4	97-1/2	United States
--	UAC 8.5	Redernes Skibskredit-Forening	*	D	1980	6	98	Norway
--	SF 30	Interfrigo	*	D	1981	5	99	Belgium
--	$20 Cdn	IBRD	I	D	1991	5-3/4	97	--
March	$15	Clark Equipment Overseas	*	CD	1981	4-1/2	100	United States
--	$27.5	Transalpine Finance Holdings	*	D	1985	6-1/2	100	--
--	$15	Government of New Zealand	*	D	1986	6-1/2	96	New Zealand
--	$20	Telefonaktiebolaget L. M. Ericcson	*	D	1986	6-1/2	97-1/2	Sweden
--	$6	Cincinnati International	*	D	1975	6-1/4	97	United States
--	$15	W. R. Grace Overseas	*	CD	1986	5	97-1/2	United States
--	$15	International Harvester	*	CD	1986	5	100	United States
--	$10	Copenhagen Telephone	*	D	1986	6-3/4	98-3/4	Denmark
--	DM 100	Thyssen Investment	*	D	1981	6-1/2	99	Germany
--	DM 100	High Veld Steel & Vanadium	*	D	1978	6-1/2	100	South Africa
--	SF 60	N. V. Philips Lamps		D	1984	5	100	The Netherlands
--	£7	Republic of Ireland	*	OD	1981	7	97-3/4	Ireland
--	Lira 12,000	Compagnie de Saint-Gobain		D	1984	6	95	France
April	$20	Continental Oil International	*	D	1971	6-3/8	99-3/4	United States

Month	Amount	Issuer		Type	Year	Rate	Price	Country
--	$35	Province of Ontario^b		D	1996	6-1/2	100	Canada
--	$59.58	Quebec Hydro-Electric Commission^b		D	1992	5-3/8	98.96	Canada
--	UAC 20	Mexican Federal Electricity	*	D	1986	6-1/2	97-1/2	Mexico
May	$25	European Investment Bank	I*	D	1976	6-1/2	98	--
--	$5	Jutland Telephone Company	*	D	1984	5-3/4	88	Denmark
--	$6	Mortgage Bank of Denmark	*	D	1971	6-1/2	100	Denmark
--	$12	International Utilities Overseas	*	CD	1986	5-1/4	97-1/2	Canada
--	$20	Bankers International	*	CD	1986	5	100	United States
--	SF 60	Esso Standard		D	1981	5	99	United States
--	SF 30	Eurofima	I	D	1983	5-1/2	100	--
June	$20	John Deere Overseas	*	CD	1986	5	100	United States
--	$10	City of Oslo		D	1976	6-3/4	98-3/4	Norway
--	$25	Cities Service International	*	D	1971	6-3/8	99-3/4	United States
--	$15	ECSC	I*	D	1978	6-1/2	99-1/2	--
--	$6	Fonds de Reetablissement de Conseil de l'Europe	I*	D	1978	6-3/4	98	--
--	$62	IBRD^b	I	D	1991	5-3/8	99.75	--
--	$30	City of Montreal^b		D	1991	5-5/8	99.65	Canada
--	$41.6	British Columbia Hydro^b		D	1991	5-5/8	98	Canada
--	DM 718.287	Deutsche Texaco	*	CD	1986	5	91.92	United States
--	SF 4.5	Huhtamaeki S.A.		D	1976	5-1/2	96-1/2	Finland
July	$15	Austrian Electricity	G*	D	1986	6-5/8	96-1/2	Austria
--	$15	EIB	I*	D	1986	6-1/2	99-1/2	--
--	$20	Transalpine Finance	*	D	1985	6-3/4	98-1/2	--
--	$15	Beecham International	*	CD	1981	5-1/2	100	United Kingdom
--	$5	Hollis Financial & Commercial	*	D	1981	6	100	The Netherlands
--	$15	Mexico State^b		D	1981	6-7/8	96-1/2	Mexico
--	DM 100	General Electric Overseas	*	D	1971	6-1/4	99-5/8	United States

TABLE 12 (Cont'd)

Date of Issue	Amount of Loan and Currency of Issue (in millions)	Name of Issue	Type of Issue[a]	Form of Issue[a]	Maturity Date	Coupon of the Loan (Nominal Interest Rate)	Issue Price	Nationality of Issuing Party
July	SF 50	ICI	I	D	1981	5-1/4	99	United Kingdom
--	Lira 15,000	EIB	I	D	1986	6	96	--
--	FF 200	EIB	I	D	1981	6-1/4	99-3/4	--
August	VAC 4.6	Hojgaard & Schultz	*	D	1973	6	96	Denmark
--	SF 50	Inter-American Development Bank	I	D	1981	5-3/4	100	United States
--	£5	Republic of Ireland	I	D	1983	7-1/2	97	Ireland
September	$9	Aktiebolaget Gotaverken	G*	D	1978	6-3/4	98	Sweden
--	$15	Brenner Autobahn	G*	D	1971	7	97-3/4	Austria
--	$10	Cabot International	*	D	1971	7	99	United States
--	$20	ENI	*	D	1981	6-1/2	97	Italy
--	$10	Government of New Zealand	*	D	1976	7	98	New Zealand
--	$25	Philips International	*	D	1976	6-3/4	99-1/4	The Netherlands
--	$34.7	Quebec Hydro-Electric[b]		D	1991	6-1/4	100	Canada
October	$20	Goodyear International	*	D	1971	6-3/4	99	United States
--	$5	Kockums Mekaniska Verkstads	G*	D	1976	6-3/4	96	Sweden
--	$15	Honeywell International	*	D	1971	6-5/8	100	United States
--	UAC 6	Sacor	*	D	1976	6-3/4	97	Portugal
--	DM 100	Siemens Europa	*	D	1981	7	100	Germany
--	SF 7	Club Mediterranee		D	1973	6	100	France
--	SF 50	Hoechst Finanz		D	1981	5-3/4	100	Germany
--	£12	Government of New Zealand		D	1986	7-1/2	98	New Zealand
--	£3	Government of Jamaica		D	1979	7-3/4	97-1/2	Jamaica
November	$13	Republic of Portugal	*	D	1976	7	98-1/2	Portugal
--	$7	Austrian Investment Bank	*	D	1971	7	97-3/4	Austria
--	$6	Andes Hydro-Electric	*	D	1981	7	97	Peru
--	$20	ECSC	I*	D	1986	6-1/2	98-1/2	--
--	$10	State of Mexico[b]		D	1981	7-1/4	96-1/2	Mexico
--	$17.5	New Brunswick Electric[b]		D	1991	6	98	Canada

--	$30	City of Montreal[b]		D	2006	6	95	Canada
--	DM 125	General Motors Overseas	*	D	1976	6-3/4	99-1/2	United States
--	DM 7.5	International Standard Electric	*	CD	1986	6		United States
--	SF 5	Hypotheken Bank des Landes Voralberg		D	1978	5-3/4	99	Germany
--	£25	Republic of Ireland		D	1986	7-1/2	99	Ireland
--	BF 500	EIB	I	D	1978	7	99	--
December	$15	Ameribas Holding	*	D	1971	6-5/8	99-1/2	--
--	$10	Sun International	*	D	1972	6-5/8	99-1/2	United States
--	$25	British Petroleum Ltd.	*	D	1978	6-3/4	99-3/4	United Kingdom
--	$25	Hercules International	*	D	1971	6-5/8	99-1/2	United States
--	$25	Commonwealth of Australia	*	D	1976	6-1/2	97-1/2	Australia
--	$3	Hollis Financial	*	D	1981	6	100	The Netherlands
--	UAC 5	CUF		D	1976	7	99	Portugal
--	UAC 10	Copenhagen Country Authority	*	D	1976	6-3/4	98	Denmark
--	SF 50	Compagnie de Saint-Gobain		D	1981	5-3/4	100	France

[a]Key:
I   an international organization
G   a government-guaranteed loan
*   an internationally syndicated loan (differentiated from a loan distributed in a small number of countries to a restricted group of investors)
D   a straight debenture issue
CD a convertible debenture issue
WD a debenture issue with warrants attached
OD a debenture issue with an optional currency clause
PD a parallel debenture issue

[b]No interest-equalization tax is payable.

[c]Actually $2.5 million plus DM 20 million in parallel.

Source: Derived from the Banking Commission of the European Economic Community.

ABOUT THE AUTHORS

John F. Chown heads his own economic and financial consulting firm, located in London, which specializes in the financial and taxation aspects of international business. Before the formation of J. F. Chown & Company Ltd. in 1962, Mr. Chown was a Director of Maxwell Stamp Associates Ltd., economic consultants. His previous experience has also included a position with a City of London firm, where he specialized in corporate mergers, and associations with firms in the United Kingdom, Canada, and West Africa. Mr. Chown has lectured widely on the subjects of banking, financial aspects of doing business abroad, taxes, and international bonds. His articles on related subjects have appeared in Moorgate & Wall Street, The Statist, The Stock Exchange Gazette, The Economist, The Times (London), and Management Today. Mr. Chown was educated at Gordonstoun and Selwyn College, Cambridge University, where he won double first-class honors in economics.

Robert Valentine is an Associate in the London office of McKinsey & Company, Inc., international management consultants. His previous experience includes consulting work with J. F. Chown & Company and with the London office of Mills Spence & Company, a leading Canadian investment organization. Mr. Valentine was graduated from Glasgow University, where he received double honors in economics and mathematics. He contributes a regular column on commodity markets to the Glasgow Herald.